BELOVED, YOU CAN WIN!

BELOVED, YOU CAN WIN!

YOU CAN WIN!

Strategies for Walking Your Talk

LINDA H. HOLLIES

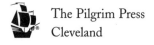

The Pilgrim Press
Cleveland

The Pilgrim Press, 700 Prospect Avenue, Cleveland, Ohio 44115-1100
thepilgrimpress.com
© 2008 by Linda H. Hollies

Lucille Clifton, "wont you celebrate with me" from *The Book of Light*.
Copyright ©1993 by Lucille Clifton. Reprinted with the permission of
Copper Canyon Press, www.coppercanyonpress.org.

Safiyah Fosua, "Remembering Coretta Scott King: April 27, 1927–January 30,
2006" copyright ©2006 The General Board of Discipleship of The United
Methodist Church. Reprinted with permission.

Scripture quotations, unless otherwise noted, are from the New Revised
Standard Version of the Bible, © 1989 by the Division of Christian Education
of the National Council of Churches of Christ in the United States of America
and are used by permission. Changes have been made for inclusivity.

♺ Printed in the United States of America on acid-free paper that contains
post-consumer fiber.

13   12   11   10   09   08   5   4   3   2   1

Library of Congress Cataloging-in-Publication Data

Hollies, Linda H.
    Beloved, you can win! : strategies for walking your talk / Linda H. Hollies.
       p. cm.
       ISBN 978-0-8298-1792-8 (alk. paper)
       1. Christian women—Religious life.   2. Christian life.   I. Title.
BV4527.H645 2008
248.4—dc22   2008005074

IN MEMORIAM

Rev. Dr. Linda H. Hollies, age sixty-four, bestselling author and United Methodist pastor, died unexpectedly on August 18, 2007, in Phoenix, Arizona. She was a prolific writer, popular speaker and a best-selling author of The Pilgrim Press, having written over one dozen books. Dr. Hollies was in Phoenix on a book publicity tour to promote *Sister, Save Yourself! Direct Talk about Domestic Violence.* She was scheduled to preach at a local church the morning she died.

A favorite word of Dr. Hollies was "bodacious," a term she frequently used in her books to empower women. The word and the ideas associated with it became so popular with her fan base that *Publishers Weekly* had this to say: "Define bodacious as 'unmistakable, remarkable, and noteworthy' and you've a good working description of Hollies."

Dr. Hollies' numerous works are best summed up in her own words, written July 11, 2007: "As a woman of color, incest survivor, clergywoman, wife, mother, and grandmother, I have taken the 'stuff' of my own life, woven it together, by God's amazing grace, and offer it to my sisters as a guide in every book. My work is intentionally self-revealing to detail how pain is fertilizer for growth into our best self."

She will be greatly missed by those who worked with her at The Pilgrim Press.

CONTENTS

PREFACE

I DIDN'T JUST DECIDE TO WRITE THIS BOOK. BUT RATHER THE Holy Spirit has decided that I'm to take this trip with the apostle Paul, and I'm so glad that you have come to journey with me for a while!

Many people know me from one of my books, *Jesus and Those Bodacious Women: Life Lessons from One Sister to Another.* It's my prayer that you have either seen, read, or heard it discussed. I'm bodacious because I am filled with the Holy Spirit, who calls me to do, to say, and to write for God's "little ones." When I was in seminary, my first New Testament professor, Dr. William Stegner, over and over again taught us, drilled us, and reminded us that as professionally trained clergy our job was not to feed the large and tall giraffes. But our task was to "put the cookies on the lower shelf so that the babes in Christ, even the wee ewe lambs, can understand and eat." This is certainly my endeavor with every message and every book that I write. It is my aim, again, in this work.

As a United Methodist pastor, I'm "sold" on following the common lectionary for my daily devotions. This means that I adhere to a predetermined set of scriptures used by my denomination across the world. In this way, it is hoped that on Mondays when our congregations return to the secular world, they might be engaged with other church-going worshipers about the taught word of God being lived out in the workplace.

Like most clergy, when I was first introduced to the lectionary, I felt it was too forced, too contrived, and too controlling. With great hesitation, however, I decided to try it. I discovered that every week, God had something new to reveal to Linda! I began to look forward to the fresh word that was going to carry me on my daily journey through life. The people in the pew only got the leftovers! For I know that God feeds me through the selected Hebrew (Old Testament) scripture; the psalm, the epistle, and the Gospel (from the first four books of the New Testament) lesson for each week.

The lectionary is not a device of only the United Methodist denomination but is used by many others as well. Years A, B, and C will take us through the entire Bible in a three-year cycle. As I write today, we are in Year C and following Genesis, Matthew, and Romans. I can't even tell you how many times I have followed this cycle and read these same scriptures. But one day recently while I was reading Romans 12, the "light bulb" came on for me! It was like God had placed this passage into my view! This means that I was going through something in my own personal life that needed work. I was going through a season where I was seeking a word of new life within my own experiences. I was hungry and open to hear God in a different way at this particular time, and this chapter became a powerful source of inspiration, education, and motivation for me. I read. I meditated. I was moved. I was not instructed to deal with the entire book of Romans. Therefore, we are now walking this particular road together utilizing Paul's winning strategies for holy, productive, effective, and practical living from one chapter, Romans chapter 12.

A word about Paul: As have most women in ordained ministry, I have had my share of "fights and arguments" with the way that the church has represented the apostle Paul. To tell me to sit and to be quiet because Paul said it rubbed me the wrong way for many years. I finally took the time, however, to invest in studying what Paul "really" said. In this latter part of my life, I'm more in agreement with him than not! It has taken a long and serious journey in order to *not* believe that Paul was against women in ministry! Paul gives too much honor, too much homage, and too much writing space detailing the working ministry of women throughout his journeys to have been "against" us.

In the book of Romans alone, Paul greets nine women! As he closes his letter to the Romans (chapter 16), he first mentions

Phoebe, whom he recommends and who is probably to be the bearer of the letter itself. He describes her as a deacon of the church at Cenchreae, "and as a benefactor of many and of myself as well"! Paul greets Prisca, Mary, Junia, Tryphaena, Tryphosa, Persis, the mother of Rufus, Julia, and the sister of Nereus. Paul singles out Prisca for her work with Paul and for risking her life; Mary for her hard work; Junia as an apostle; Tryphaena, Tryphosa, and Persis for their labor. Nothing in Paul's comments justifies the conclusion that these women worked in ways that differed either in kind or in quantity from the ways in which men worked. All of the individuals listed appear to be engaged in tasks of ministry, a fact that needs to be taken into account in any assessment of the roles of women in early Christianity."[1]

So Paul, this great man of God, was not "against" women in the church. He was against the death of people in the church! This great giant of the faith, who was called to win gentiles to the Way, came to confront all of the "worldly and fleshly wisdom" of the Roman and Greek world. This man of God had been knocked off his high horse, blinded, and taken into a strange home where he could "hear" from God directly. Paul knew that he was off on a rough journey. Paul realized that his message was not going to be easy, soothing, and well received. But Paul was a man on a mission to win souls for Jesus Christ by setting the record straight, which he did both by direct communications and by putting his pen to paper in letter form. Not only did Paul want to win souls and erect new churches, Paul wanted the folk to stay on the "straight path."

I recognize that I am the light of the world. My light, given to me by God, before my birth, is mine to use, to shine, and to spread. Like Paul, I was sent into this world to make a permanent, positive impact and to effect change! So I'm a candle, a light, a bright burning "Son" beam. Every place that I go is affected by my light. Everyone that I come in contact with experiences my radiance. The more gloom that there is around me, the more my light will shine. And the more my light shines, the better I feel.

Know that I have not always been this way! I can vividly recall one occasion when the gloom got really thick. The going got very rough. So I decided to take a hike, run out of the meeting, get into my car, and head home! But when I turned the key to start my car, my CD player began to play. As I drove down the road, I began singing along, "If you can use anything, God, you can use me."[2] And the Holy Spirit gently asked, "How can I use you if you're going to run away?" I had to turn my car around, abolish all my plans to sulk at the mall, and go back to the meeting and be reconciled with my sisters and brothers, who were looking for me when I returned.

Conditions, circumstance, and situations continue to come, but they cannot deter, they cannot turn off my light, and they cannot prevent my light from shining. I have grown with the help of the Holy Spirit. My role in life is to help my sisters and my brothers to find "the possible" in every seemingly impossible situation. My task on the journey is to help others seek and find their inherent spiritual powers that are already placed within each of us by God. For all that we need has been supplied by the resurrection of Jesus Christ and is waiting to be sharpened and strengthened through the wind, the fire, and the dynamic power of the Holy Spirit!

One of my greatest thrills is to teach, preach, and practice Holy Spirit living! The Holy Spirit has empowered me to discover, to develop, and to deploy my spiritual gifts. I believe that when we know and walk in our spiritual gifts, the world of division, envy, and low self-esteem will hasten to an end. My spiritual gifts are those of faith, administration, being a pastor-teacher, and encouraging the people of God.

I have been commissioned to birth this book into our world to help defuse the failure mechanism that speaks so loudly in our ears. I'm assigned to pump you up by the power of the Holy Spirit! My job is to prime your spiritual pump, to feed your mind, and to stir your spirit so that you will have more practical advice, better understanding, and clearer wisdom about how to go forth, effective and powerful on your walk of faith into holy bodaciousness!

Our God has no respect of person. What God has done for others, God is ready to do for you too. God's arms are not too short to reach you. God's ears are not closed to hear your cries for movement. God's desires to help you are greater than your desires to be helped. So let's prepare our hearts and minds for bodacious living with the apostle Paul's practical application of holy living found within these verses.

Author's Note about Scripture

For my own personal study and reflection, I generally use two different translations of the Bible. I favor both the New International Version (NIV) and *The Message: The Bible in Contemporary Language*, (though I do not limit myself to those versions). I shift between versions, including the New Revised Standard Version favored by the publisher. Of course, the NIV sounds much like our familiar King James Version (KJV), with better language use, while Eugene Peterson's *The Message* uses today's words and statements. So don't hesitate to have your own personal Bible close to you while reading, studying, or meditating with this book.

Due to the patriarchal structure of the world in the days of Bible construction, during book selection for the canon, and even today—I find the primarily male dominant language to be stifling for me. Therefore, I take great liberty to "translate," or paraphrase parts of scripture to include those of my gender. This is not an apology, but just a note so that you will not be surprised, shocked, or appalled when you cannot find the "exact" version of a passage in your Bible. You will find what I felt—that the Bible was intended for the whole people of God.

At the beginnings of this book's chapters, I include a verse in my words and understanding, and then follow it with one from one of the Bible translations. As I worked with the Romans 12 passage, I did elect to add the endearing term "Beloved" in front of each verse. This word was one that apostle Paul sometimes used as he addressed his audience, attempting to show his readers and hearers just how close to his heart they were. This is my foremost intent as I write to you. Beloved, I want you to know that we are on a journey toward a wonderful destination, and we will get there, one day, one step at a time! Be encouraged, Beloved, for we can win!

Seven Steps to Bodacious Living

I want to begin with my seven personal steps for living as bodacious and effective Christians:

1. *Give up what "Mama 'n 'em" told you as a child.* Ordinary, go-along-to-get-along, do-the-minimum-and-don't-get-too-noticed will no longer work! Old, ordinary thinking, politically correct practice has got to go! We have to learn how to walk, talk, and live by faith. We have to reprogram our minds, our thinking, and our language into God's way. We have to learn how to dream bigger dreams. We have to learn how to set larger goals. We have to learn how to stretch ourselves and to think outside of the box. What I'm trying to say is that we have to come to wholly depend upon an incomprehensible God! The written word of God and that inward desire to grow spiritually and to have an open mind to hear what the Spirit is saying to you will provide so much more than "Mama 'n 'em" ever dreamed possible. Give up what "Mama 'n 'em" told you and let's walk in a maturing faith, relying solely on reading, rehearsing, and repeating God's Word so that we grow into our destiny.

2. *Decide, declare, and decree, "I'm going to experience the abundant life!"* Say it! Mean it! We decide with our mind. We declare with our mouth. And we decree by the authority of the Holy Spirit a thing into being. So decide, declare, and decree that you are going to be open and available for much more than you know or think. Be on the lookout for next. Anticipate the best. And always strive for excellence. Be allergic to negative people, places, and things. Separate, come out from among the down-talking, down-living, can't-see-nothing-better people who want to keep you down with them! Realize, understand, and fully comprehend that everybody does not want to see you move on up! Too many folks are praying for you to stay down and to even go further down, so that they can feel good about themselves. Decide. Declare. Decree. "I'm going

to use my energies to enlarge my mind and my territory. For I'm going to experience the abundant life!"

3. *Change your mind! Shake off old limiting thoughts.* Rid yourself of old negative habits and begin to acquire healthy and helpful habits. Stop using old negative language when you speak and begin to use words of wisdom and empowerment. Stop being resentful and learn how to forgive. Let go of yesterday. Forget it. Get over it. Just ask to the Savior to help you! When we decide to change our minds, our life will change for the better. Bless, not curse. Pray, not fight. Love, not hate. Forgive, and do not hold grudges. Consciously decide to change your mind. Make different decisions. Learn from old and ancient pain and then—move on!

4. *Find some new "high steppers" to hang with.* Meet and network with people who are on the road to somewhere! And definitely dress for where you want to go. Find two others ready for bodacious living. When there are two or three who can touch and agree, a blessing, affirming, positive trinity will increase your path to bodacious living exponentially. Let me tell you about my Monday Morning Prayer Group of Sisters! Let me share with you about my Thursday afternoon group of lectionary preachers. As we met around Holy Scriptures, we would discuss, dialogue, argue, and agree to disagree but, nevertheless, we loved one another. It was effectiveness enhanced. It was energy restored. It was blessings shared. I pray that by now you have caller ID and voice mail on your phone. So, now, delete low steppers from your life.

5. *Seek council from your teammates.* Be honest and practice saying, "I don't know." Practice asking, "What do you think about this?" Practice asking, "How does this sound to you?" Honest people will help you to stretch your vision. Honest people will help you to create bigger, better, and more effective dreams. And honest people will be your prayer support and your encouragers as you journey to the land of bodacious living!

6. *Let go of your anticipated and expected outcomes.* Trust the process of daily living and allow God to order your steps. To "let go and let God" be in charge is a solid plan for bodacious living. Trust the process. It is well!

7. *Finally, give yourself away! Let your light shine.* Offer. Share. Serve. Give. Harm no one. Speak ill of no one. Speak love to all. Think love of all. Walk in love in all that you do. Love heals. Love transforms. Love changes. Love conquers. Love is divine. Love is bodacious.

Go forth into the world with a spirit of excellence in all that you do. You are the light of the world wherever you are. As light, the very personal representative of Jesus Christ, you are here to heal, to transform, to bring love, harmony, and good will. Rather than trying to impose your will upon others, or even feeling that you have to teach others, simply choose to think, feel, and live in the light of God as the light of God. When you come to know, through your interior ally, that you are the light, you don't need permission from the world to shine. The light of God within you will release you from the negative forces that seek to hinder you, to stifle you, and to keep you bound.

I'm thankful to Mrs. Minnie Gibson, who was a member of the congregation when I was pastor at Southlawn United Methodist Church, in Chicago, Illinois. One Sunday morning she challenged us who were singing with gusto "Jesus Is the Light of the World!" She reminded us that "we" are the lights of the world! "We" are the salt. "We" are the cities that set up on a hill for the world to see, to notice, and to emulate! I've been singing the song "correctly" since that Sunday!

Beloved, you can win! God has so much in store for our lives that it would honestly blow our minds if we could see it. But for now, we are only responsible for doing what we know. So let's prepare to rehearse what we know and then add to our knowledge base of walking our Christian talk. I'm on the journey with you!

Let's pray, one for the other! Shalom!

INTRODUCTION

won't you celebrate with me
what i have shaped into
a kind of life? i had no model.
born in babylon
both nonwhite and woman
what did i see to be except myself?
i made it up
here on this bridge between
star shine and clay,
my one hand holding tight
my other hand; come celebrate
with me that everyday
something has tried to kill me
and has failed. . . .[1]

—Lucille Clifton

THIS *IS* THE ERA OF THE HOLY SPIRIT!

When I was a child, growing up in the black community of Gary, Indiana, there were a number of ways we used to describe us. These names were indications of who and what you were in the community. If you were a flirtatious and cute male, you were called "mannish." If you were female, with the same tendencies, you were called "fast." If you had accumulated a little something, had a job, house, and car, you were a "big Negro." If you were making it along on meager fare, you were called a "little Negro." But, the worst thing that anybody could be called in my neighborhood was a "no-account Negro"! For if it was judged that you simply ain't "no count," it meant that you didn't factor into the equation of black life. It meant that your person and your presence were not important; basically, you were nonessential. To be called "no count" signified that as a person you were inconsequential. You didn't matter, you didn't make a difference, and you were counted out.

The first church of Jesus knew about being counted out. The disciples that Jesus had chosen, a group of stinking fishermen, some political zealots, and a tax collector, each had first-hand knowledge of being considered "no account." Every woman who followed Jesus and had gathered with the 120 in the Upper Room were especially familiar with being left out of any count. And, though we have leaped forward almost 2006 years and consider ourselves to be progressive, enlightened, and modern, we are not very much different from that first group of Christians. Have you ever had the experience of being crossed out, bypassed, written off, overlooked, excluded, "dissed," kicked to the curb, and treated as if you simply did not count? It's not a good feeling!

It ought not be too surprising to us when we consider that God's own son had first-hand experience with being considered a "no account." He was born in a manger, not a mansion. He didn't start out his life as royalty in Europe, but was forced to flee to Africa as a refugee. The neighborhood where he was raised was so remote, so country, that "city folks" all asked, "Can anything good come out of Nazareth?" Although he made the world and created the universe, he declared that "foxes have holes, birds have nests, but the son of man has nowhere to lay his head." Jesus was a card-carrying member of the "no account club."

But—this word makes the greatest difference—*but*—this word that indicates that something important is about to follow—*but*—this word that says, watch out for the punch *line*—*but* Jesus, a member of the "no account" club, *made a difference!* And, his living, dying, rising again, and sending us the gift of the Holy

Spirit to live within us says that everyone of us does count. We can make a difference and, when the world writes us off, it is the Holy Spirit who writes us back into the game of life. "Repent and be baptized, every one of you, in the name of Jesus Christ for the forgiveness of your sins. And you will receive the gift of the Holy Spirit" (Acts 2:38).

The woman with the issue of blood had been written off. *But* after twelve long years, she touched the hem of his garment and was made whole. He counted her back in. The man who laid by the pool of Bethesda had been counted out. *But* after thirty-eight long years, Jesus spoke to him and counted him back in. Lazarus had certainly been counted out. Dead and stinking for four whole days, *but, but, but* . . . Jesus, who came late, was right on time in counting him back in! Jesus has a habit of including the excluded, writing in those who have been written off, and counting in those who have been counted out! I am so very glad that Jesus came!

And, then, on the Day of Pentecost, Jesus proved to a group of folks that they did count. It didn't matter that the rest of the world felt they were unimportant. It didn't make any difference that they had internalized the feelings of not being significant. It was not critical that they had blown it, failed, doubted, run away, hidden, and messed up! What was of great consequence was the fact that they had obeyed his command to come together. They were all physically together in one place, because we need each other. We cannot make it by ourselves. We need each other for support. We need each other for encouragement. We need each other for prayer and fellowship. We are only as strong as the weakest one in our midst. And most of us are going through, trying to hold on by the hairs on our chinny-chin-chins. We need each other to prop us up on every leaning side, for we are simply dirt. We are just creatures made out of earth.

When the storms of life begin to rage, and the booming sound of thunder begins to roll, you can see pieces of earth being picked up, moved, swept along, rearranged, and relocated. For earth is not stable. Earth is frail, delicate, and subject to being disturbed. So earth has to have something to cling to, to stick with, and to hold onto in the rough times. Like it or not, we need to come together. When you are going through, it's not the time to stay away from the community of faith. When the going gets rough, it's not the time to pull away from those who want to help you hold steady. When you're being kicked in the teeth by the world, you need to have a place and a people you can run to for refuge. So, when your world is falling apart and you can't hold things together, find your way to the house of God. For good things happen when God's people come together.

The people of God were together emotionally. Individually, they had each been wounded by the wider community. Individually, each one of them had been affected by the death and seeming loss of their beloved teacher. But when they came together, wounded hearts were renewed. When they came together, aching spirits were helped. When they came together, individual hopelessness turned to community optimism. For good things happen when God's people come together.

When you can't see the sunshine, somebody in the community will testify, "I know the Lord will make a way somehow." When you can't lift your voice and sing, somebody will break out with "Jesus is the center of my joy. He's both my music and my song." When you feel as if nobody cares, somebody will declare, "Jesus loves me, this I know, for the Bible tells me so!" When you dare to bring your hurts, your failures, and your disappointments and gather with the people of God, something good happens. When you leave the community of God's people, you know that the sun will rise again. When you leave, you can have that blessed assurance that you won't be in the pit always. When you leave, you will have the firm conviction that a new day is going to dawn for you. Friends, there is healing for everything that ails us when we come together under the power and anointing of the Holy Spirit!

What we need to remember is that these sisters and brothers were together spiritually, for they had heard the sound as of violent wind. Then they saw divided tongues, as of fire, and the Holy Spirit rushed in and sat upon each of them. Do you get the message that the elements of wind and fire came to mix with and to mess with common earth? You know what happens when wind and earth meet and mix. You get a whirling mass of energy. You get a shift in perspective. And you get movement in a new direction. When fire and earth meet, a combustion occurs. You get an explosion. For the three elements are not compatible. So a dynamic force is created. When earth, wind, and fire come together you have the potential for tornadoes, whirlwinds, and hurricanes. When earth, wind, and fire come together, the velocity and energy created demands transformation. Things cannot remain the same.

With the rushing in of the Holy Spirit, sounding like wind and looking like fire, the "no accounts" shifted to the winning side. With the rushing in of the Holy Spirit, filling in the blanks, filling up the empty spaces, and empowering this group for the ministry of mission, these, who the world had written off, began to write a whole new chapter about God. With the rushing in of the Holy Spirit and a touch of wind and fire on these creatures of earth, their potential was released; their capabilities were enhanced and their possibilities were multiplied.

Today, the people of the world need to be on the alert to the ones they've discounted and written off. The church needs to be on the lookout for a fresh touch of the wind and the fire, which comes to give us new energy and empowers us to move out and change the world for God. There is a perfect remedy yet available for those who have been counted out. It makes no difference whether the world counted you out or whether you counted yourself out; the wind and the fire of the Holy Spirit are available to touch us. The wind and the fire of the Holy Spirit are present to refresh us. The wind and the fire of the Holy Spirit will assist us to meet and to overcome every storm in our lives.

Earth, wind and fire met in that Upper Room, for they were brought together by the power and the promise of the resurrected and ascended Christ. They found out that Jesus needed them to count. We are the only tools, the only voices, the only feet, and the only hands that move the realm of God forward. Beloved, Jesus needs you! Honey Child, Jesus needs your spiritual gifts at work performing daily ministry. Precious, Jesus needs your dollars to keep the doors of healing stations open around the world in order that people can come together when our personal worlds are falling apart. Dear One, Jesus needs us to work together in mission ministry, supporting each other and our outreach to a dying world. Friend of Mine, Jesus needs you and me to make the personal calls, send the wonderful cards, do the pastoral visits, and pray for each other. Church, Jesus needs us to count. We also must make a difference in the world and be accountable to each other!

There are so many options God could have used. There are so many directions God could have chosen. I don't know why the Trinity chose to use particles of earth to be filled with fire and the force of the wind to change, transform, and win the lost. But I'm so glad God chose me. I know that when most people look at me they put me on the "no account" list. They ask questions like, "Who does she think she is?" I fully understand that short, dark-skinned women are not the most highly valued commodities in the world. And I have come to comprehend that too many people discount preachers and feel that the church is way behind the times. *But, but, but* I read the end of the story! I cheated and went to the back of the book!

I saw seven churches with seven angels, and I saw four and twenty angels. I didn't count in those numbers. I read on and saw one hundred and twenty-four thousand. I didn't count in those numbers. But around the throne of God there was a number that could not be counted.

The earth creatures had come from every nation, every tribe, every people, and every tongue. They will never hunger or thirst again. They will never die again. They will never have to feel disappointment or cry again. For God has promised to wipe all of their tears away. John asked the angel, "who are these, and where did they come from?" The angel informed John that these were simply lumps of dirt who had been touched by wind and baptized by fire. "These are they who have come through great tribulation and washed their robes in the blood of the Lamb."

I'm in that number. I count! And, I'm going to hold onto God's unchanging hand. I'm going to continue to pray and to ask the wind to blow on me and the fire to fall on me, afresh and anew. I am determined to keep on making a difference. I am persuaded that I can make things happen. I am serious about being a change agent for Jesus Christ. I want to count for the long haul. It's promised that earth, wind, and fire will meet again! Don't hesitate to be in the number. Thanks be unto God for the precious gift of the Holy Spirit, who works in us, through us, and often in spite of us to help us walk the talk of Christian living!

The full purpose of this work is to help each of us to put our talk and our walk of Christian living together. The full purpose of this work is to provide practice, day-by-day activities that will make God proud, the devil defeated, and the realm of God advance! We can no longer play church! The time has come when the world is seeking answers, searching for paths to meaning, purpose, and destiny. It's time for us to be the evidence that we claim with our tall steeples, our megachurches, and our huge crosses! The time for cheap talk and cheap discipleship is over. Years ago, Dietrich Bonhoeffer, a German theologian, questioned where the "church" was as Hitler was diligently exterminating Jews and the Christians throughout the world were silent. Listen to what he had to say then:

> Cheap grace is the preaching of forgiveness without requiring repentance, baptism without church discipline, Communion without confession, absolution without personal confession. Cheap grace is grace without discipleship, grace without the cross, grace without Jesus Christ, living and incarnate.
>
> Costly grace is the treasure hidden in the field; for the sake of it [one] will gladly go and sell all that [one] has. It is the pearl of great price to buy which the merchant will sell all his [or her] goods. It is the . . . rule of Christ, for whose sake [one] will pluck out the eye which

causes [one] to stumble; it is the call of Jesus Christ at which the disciple leaves his nets and follows him.

Costly grace is the gospel which must be *sought* again and again, the gift which must be *asked* for, the door at which [one] must *knock*.

Such grace is *costly* because it calls us to follow.... It is costly because it costs [one one's] life, and it is grace because it gives [one] the only true life. It is costly because it condemns sin, and grace because it justifies the sinner. Above all, it is *costly* because it cost God the life of [the Beloved] Son: "ye were bought at a price," and what has cost God so much cannot be cheap for us. Above all, it is *grace* because God did not reckon [the Beloved] Son too dear a price to pay for our life, but delivered him up for us.

Costly grace is the Incarnation of God.[2]

The time has come for the church to put up! The time for play, pretense, and posturing is over! There are wars and rumors of wars; there is HIV/AIDS running rampant in Africa but also here in our country; there is poverty, in a continuing down-spiraling economy; our young people are lost, fishing for religion and a way out of their misery; and the boomers, gen-Xers, as well as older adult people are looking for the reality of the true and the living God! We must be their living Bibles!

This is not a new message. This is not a get-quick scheme. This is not some plot about bigger and better or even getting more. This is the same old message that Paul taught to the first church about practical application for their lives in the world. This is the relentless apostle's understanding of how we ought to walk the talk of following the One who gave his life as a ransom for us. Sometimes, I just believe that we need to "hear" the old story in a different voice. So, Beloved, I present to you some old, but effective, winning strategies for Christian living! Remember this is the dispensation, the era, and the reign of the Holy Spirit! Let's all sing, "Spirit of the Living God, fall afresh on me!"

Beloved's Personal Journey

Paul, who became a commissioned apostle sent to win the gentile community to Jesus Christ, was a man of great commitment. He saw himself as a "servant, a slave" to the good news. He knew, recognized, and appreciated that he had been bought with a price; that of the redeeming blood of Calvary. Paul was determined to encounter any error of doctrine with powerful truth. He assured his readers, his listeners, and his peers that they were not simply dealing with a mere man, but a man filled with the power of the Holy Spirit's authority. He was well aware of his destiny, his divine purpose, and his call to preach truth, even to power.

1. When were you introduced to the Holy Spirit?

2. Have you taken a personal spiritual gifts survey to discover your special grace in the body of Christ? Name your top three spiritual gifts.

3. How would you describe "cheap grace" to someone?

4. When does your local congregation celebrate the arrival of the Holy Spirit, or Pentecost, to the people of God?

5. Is there a ministry at your local church that teaches members about how to discover their spiritual gifts? What tools do they utilize?

6. What is your personal goal for deployment of your spiritual gifts in the world?

7. Say a prayer of thanks to the Holy Spirit who leads, guides, and directs your steps.

1

TRANSFORMED BY TROUBLE

*Do everything in life by placing
it before God as your personal offering.*

L. H.

*I urge you, Beloved, in view of God's mercy,
to offer your bodies as living sacrifices, holy and pleasing
to God—this is your spiritual act of worship.*

Romans 12:1 NIV

*Take your everyday, ordinary life—your sleeping,
eating, going-to-work, and walking-around life—and place
it before God as an offering, a present. Embracing what God
does for you is the best thing that you can do for God.*

Romans 12:1 The Message

WE MIGHT NOT WANT TO SHARE OUR STORIES. WE MIGHT HOPE that others don't know and never discover our stories. We might wear a mask, live a lie, pretend, and behave as if we don't have stories to tell. But the reality is that each one of us knows how it is to be transformed by the troubles that we have seen. For the world is filled with stories about women. We know the fiction, the fantasies, the great love, the comedies, the horror, and the desperate stories of many women. Yet, nobody knows the trouble I have seen, nobody but Jesus. So I know that you, too, have a story to tell.

I have been watching on television a story about five women. It's a story called *Desperate Housewives*. These are not saved, church-

1

going, Holy Spirit filled women, so I'm sure that none of you know the stories of these five women. Allow me a few minutes to share with you part of their story lines from a recent season.

First, there is Bree, a prim, proper, very upstanding wife, mother of a boy and a girl, who became a widow. She is the epitome of a dutiful, regal looking, and good housewife.

Then there is Gabby, a married slut. She is beautiful, shapely, a former model who sought sexual thrills with the young man who mowed the lawn. That was last season. This season she fell down the stairs and lost the child. And her good-looking, wealthy spouse has served time in prison.

There is Susan, an author who is a single mother with a daughter. She is financially well off, but her emotional issues have made her the award winning star of the series. She seems fairly stable, but one day we found her running down the street, crying, in a beautiful white wedding gown, as her live-in boyfriend drove away in anger. It seems that she wanted him to accept her child, but, she had serious issues with his crazy son.

There is Lynette, a married attorney with a spouse and four children. Her husband has become the stay-at-home father, while she tries to juggle her work and her life. Lynette is struggling like all of us to handle these diverse roles.

Finally, there is a black woman, Ms. Betty, who could afford to move onto Wisteria Lane. She is a single woman, highly educated, with a career as a professional pianist behind her. She proudly shows off her one son, who enjoys looking at the white daughter of a neighbor. But she has another son, who is both retarded and has killed somebody, chained in her basement.

Five different woman with stories. There are five different, conflicting, competing, and very real stories for our entertainment every Sunday night. We discover five different women with five different ways, strategies, and methods of trying to hold their respective lives together. These five distinct personalities tend to portray an element of each one of our lives. For if truth be told, each one of the women looks good on the outside, but on the inside there is much unseen and complex trouble brewing, ready to explode.

It makes no difference how we look, where we live, what we drive, who we are married to, how our children behave in front of us, or what positions we hold—trouble is always present! Or trouble just left our home, or at least, trouble is looking for us. Remember in the book of Job that Satan was going "to and fro in the earth," seeking some God-loving person to destroy. And guess who offered up Job's name?

It was God who pointed out the saved, sanctified, praying, interceding, upstanding, and righteous man to Satan. "Have you considered my servant, Job?" God sent trouble to Job in order to transform his life. Most of us think that we would like to have lives of no trouble, but then, that would be a fairy tale. For in real life, in human life, and especially in saved life, trouble will find us to help us to see exactly what it is that we're working with! Most of us know Christian talk. But trouble comes to see if we know how to walk the Christian walk. Remember to put your name in this blank: "Have you considered my servant, _____?"

Perhaps you can identify with Bree, with your hair all tidy, your house all clean, and your meals done perfectly. You will yet have troubles. Bree has a son who is a teenaged homosexual who is not in the closet. One Sunday he said to his male friend, "I hate her. When she found out that I liked boys, she sent me to counseling and told me that I was going to hell. When she finds out that I can't change, she'll hate me. So I hate her first. And I'm going to bring her down." Trouble is in Bree's house. It will transform her life. Someone with the spiritual gifts of discernment, encouragement, and exhortation needs to meet with Bree.

Perhaps you can identify with Gabby, because we have many unholy hussies in the church. There are a group of women who have not made a decision to live wholly for God, but keep sharing themselves with others, outside of a marriage covenant. It may be politically correct and "new day" acceptable, but it is unholy. And we are discovering more and more about HIV/AIDS from our sexual liaisons with men who are on the down low. That includes some of the males in the church too. So when we engage in sex outside of the marriage covenant, trouble is going to transform us. It just might kill us too! Someone with the spiritual gifts of mercy, exhortation, and pastoring-teaching needs to encounter Gabby.

Many women today can identify with Susan, who is financially independent and owns her own home. But Susan's troubles center on her need to seek counsel from her teenaged daughter. Girlfriend, that's asking for trouble. For the parent is the one with the experience. The parent is the one who is to establish guidelines, rules, and regulations. But Susan keeps letting her daughter in on her dating life, asking her opinion about adult affairs, and trouble is waiting to happen. Oh, how someone with the spiritual gifts of encouragement, mercy, and exhortation needs to have a conversation with this poor soul.

Some of us can well identify with Lynette. She wants to have it all. She gave up her career to be a stay-at-home wife. But she didn't know how not to meddle in her husband's work affairs. So he quit his job and told her to go back to work and to support them all. Trouble knocked and Lynette answered the door. For this arrangement is not working well for a mother with small children and a man who has few parenting skills. Trouble always brews whenever we find a woman taking care of a man who refuses to work. For my Bible says, "If you don't work, you don't eat." Too many women are like poor Lynette. Let those who are gifted in the art of counseling, giving spiritual and godly wisdom, step to the plate.

Finally, there is our ed black sister on Wisteria Lane. Ms. Betty feels that she has all of the answers. Her retarded son killed a white girl in the city. That's why they moved into their new home during the night. But Betty did not read that passage that says, "What's done in the dark will be shouted from the rooftop." So Betty came on the show with her secrets. Betty chained her retarded son in the basement of the house, thinking that she could control his destiny. But secrets always lead to trouble. And trouble won't stay confined to our house. The series writers have had the retarded son made a break for the outside. Trouble is about to reform Ms. Betty! Immediately, we need some good people of God who can offer the spiritual gifts of exhortation, mercy, wisdom, and pastoring-teaching to go and knock on Betty's door!

Many of us have sick children in our homes. Many of us have drug-addicted children, stealing children, sexually promiscuous children, lying and slick children, whom we won't even require to attend worship, living in our homes! We turn our backs; we close our eyes; we keep quiet and deny that there is trouble brewing. But the call for this day, the purpose of our being community, and the plan of God is for the spiritual gifts of the community to help each one of us to face our troubles. We are to go through the troubles with the help of God and to be transformed into presents fitted for holy service unto God.

God will not allow us to remain desperate! God is calling you and me to a higher level of living. God is requiring that our troubles not defeat us, but transform us, so that we might help others with our stories of being delivered. The book of Romans is a quality resource guide. For Paul declares to us that in using our everyday, walkabout lives, we can tap into the power of the Holy Spirit so that we can "rejoice with those who rejoice and weep with those who weep." Paul wanted the folk to stay on the "straight path" and to be transformed by the renewing of their minds, to be equipped by the power of their spiritual gifts and not by the mentality of the Roman way, which was powerful, cultural, and intellectual in its own eyes.

Read the words of Roman 12:1–2 in *The Message* translation. Paul writes and declares to the church in Rome:

> So here's what I want you to do, God helping you: Take your everyday, ordinary life—your sleeping, eating, going-to-work, and walking-around life—and place it before God as an offering. Embracing what God does for you is the best thing you can do for God. Don't become so well-adjusted to your culture that you fit into it without even thinking. Instead, fix your attention on God. You'll be changed from the inside out. Readily rec-

ognize what God wants from you, and quickly respond to it. Unlike the culture around you, always dragging you down to its level of immaturity, God brings the best out of you, develops well-formed maturity in you.

Remember me telling you how I was transformed by my own personal trouble and had to turn my car around, abolish all my plans to sulk at the mall, and go back to the meeting and be reconciled with my sisters and brothers? I was transformed by that troubled situation to allow God's light to shine through me.

When I think of love that is transforming, changing, divine, and bodacious, I can think of no one better than Mary, the mother of Jesus. Mary is the epitome of a woman who was transformed by trouble. Mary's transformation has now impacted the whole wide world. The first three words of Luke 2:7 declare, "And Mary gave. . . . " Talk about trouble! She was a young, single virgin. The penalty for sex before marriage was being stoned to death. Yet, Mary gave her consent to participate in creating the first Christmas day. Mary became fully engaged in the act of birthing love into a cold and evil world. Mary made a significant contribution by offering her womb to the Great I Am. She was willing to present what she possessed into partnership with the plan of God.

Mary gave up ownership of her body and blood to become the hostess to the Living Word, who ate from her body's nourishment. When the scripture records that "Mary gave . . . ," it stipulates that she gave over to God the fullness of her very self. Mary put her whole self into the mix! She withheld nothing. It was the greatest gift she could have offered. For with her giving God her "Yes," she put her life at risk.

In the middle of an era when others thought that they were forgotten by God, an angel showed up to tell Mary, "Hail, Mary, you are full of grace." Mary had found favor with God. Mary had been selected out of all the young, Jewish virgins in the land to bear the son of God. Mary was engaged to be married to Joseph. It is without doubt that she had plans, dreams, ideas, and hopes for her life. But when Mary said "yes," knowing that her life would be not simply questioned, but put on the line to face death, she was willing to put the fate of the world into her womb. The song of Mary, after she was greeted and saluted by her cousin, Elizabeth, talks about the insignificant being raised to new heights and those in power being pulled down. Mary sang a song of realization that many were weeping while others rejoiced over their down times. Mary recognized that there were those who had no joy and felt that they had no hope. So Mary gave what she had to offer to God. Mary presented her womb as a spiritual gift to the world. Today we celebrate the gift that she gave.

The Christmas story is not one that we simply rehearse every year. The Christmas story is too big, too large, too significant for us to think that we can get away with just hearing it during the Advent season! We are called to live it out in our individual lives! As Mary gave her all to God, you and I are called to do the very same thing. Giving material "gifts" to others means absolutely nothing if we have not "given" our whole selves unto the salvation of Mary's Little Lamb.

"And Mary gave birth to her firstborn, a son. She wrapped him in swaddling cloths and placed him in a manger, because there was no room for them in the inn." Mary not only gave herself as an offering, she went all the way through the birthing process. Then she took gentle care of the infant by holding him, touching him, loving him, protecting him, and wrapping him in clean cloths to help him live. Before he could offer and give us abundant life on Calvary, Mary had to provide it for him. Now, that's good news!

As non-Catholics we tend to put Sista Mary away until Advent. Most of us don't hear sermons on her offering. We need to recognize, however, that she, who allowed her trouble to transform our world, represents the church of God. That's the challenge for each one of us! Mary's example of offering and giving, providing a softness within us for Jesus Christ, is expected in our daily lives. For Mary's baby is coming back. But he won't be a tiny, helpless baby that we smile at. Jesus is coming back as the mighty Ruler of Glory, and he'll be looking for those who are in desperate love with him! Be transformed by your troubles and you can meet him in the air!

Dearly Beloved, I encourage you to be so desperately in love with Jesus Christ that you will make the necessary changes, one at a time, so that you are the very best gift that Jesus has ever received! "Take your everyday, ordinary life—your sleeping, eating, going to work and walking around life—and place it before God as an offering, a present." May the power of the Holy Spirit cause it to begin within you now and forever more!

Beloved's Personal Journey

The apostle Paul is clear that Christians are to have a high sense of moral values and ethics. We demonstrate our allegiance to Jesus Christ by "presenting" our bodies as temples of the Holy Spirit, by not conforming to the world's popular opinion, and by allowing our minds to be changed, made new and different by the transformation of the Holy Spirit within us. In Old Testament times, people were commanded to purchase their sin offering, bring it to the priest, and offer it in repentance. This posture requires that the individual does something in exchange for the ritual of being forgiven, cleansed, and acceptable to God.

1. Currently, what is the "secret" that is troubling you in your walk with Jesus Christ?

2. Can this "trouble" be a call from Jesus Christ for you to make a change in your life?

3. How can you offer this trouble to God as a personal, individual sacrifice?

4. When have you been transformed by a troubling situation before?

5. When will you put the doctrinal principles of apostle Paul into personal application for your life?

6. Write your personal goal and a prayer for walking your talk.

2

DISCERNING THE SPIRITS

*Fix your attention on God and be changed
from the inside out! Don't make the surrounding
culture your guiding force or role model.*

L. H.

*Beloved, do not conform any longer to the pattern
of this world, but be transformed by the renewing of your mind.
Then you will be able to test and approve what God's will is—
God's good, pleasing and perfect will [for your life].*

Romans 12:2 NIV

ONCE UPON A TIME, I WANTED TO BE A NURSE. IN MIDDLE school, I read every book about Cherry, the nurse. I met Cherry when she was in high school and followed her into nursing school. Cherry was white and lived in the suburbs. I was black and lived in the hood, but we were both going to be nurses. Nurses were helpful people, always assisting and being part of a healing team. The starched white uniform and that sassy little white hat probably had much attraction for me as a teenager, too. I mean, early on, my decision was made. I was going to be a nurse.

In college, however, my nursing career flew right out of the window. Physiology required the dissecting of a dog. I'd barely been able to handle the high school lab and the little frog. A dog was simply out of the question. So I dropped that course, bid farewell to nursing, and entered the field of secondary education.

Little did I know that my desire for nursing was part of God's plan, purpose, and destiny for my life. Back then, I didn't understand that God had already ordered my steps and that both diagnosing and healing were in my blood.

Today, I have an earned doctorate in ministry. I specialized in pastoral care, completing a two-year clinical residency. As a pastor, I'm a heart specialist, if you will, with a focus on the discerning of spirits. My professional career in ministry has taught me that the church is to be the hospital for the people of God. It makes no difference about our role in life, our educational achievements, or our economic status. The fact remains that we, in the church, are some sick people. I didn't say that some of us are sick. I didn't say that many of us are sick. I said that we are some sick people in God's church. Our nation is sick. Our government is sick. Our school system is sick. Our family structures are sick. This makes God's church an institution for the sick!

Instead of the church setting the standards and marching boldly into risky endeavors for God, we will reflect the culture and go along with the world's agenda—and then try to get God to bless our mess. The church of God always runs about twenty-five years behind the world in trying to keep up, but we do try to bring the business of the world into the church. No wonder we are sick! More than thirty years ago, the world got into the touchy-feely area of emotions and declared, "I'm ok. You're ok." And the church began to take the words "sin and confession" out of our vocabulary and off our worship bulletins. The world then decided that a corporate image, a logo, and a boardroom with a CEO was the standard. The church said, we need a business administrator, a pastor who can serve as our public relations person, and we need a boardroom. Now the world is talking about vision, teamwork, and diversity, stealing the very language that we have allowed to die! I told you that we are sick!

So God established the church as the hospital, the place where sick people go to be made better. The church, composed of sick people trying to keep pace in the world, is the place where we come seeking medicine for our sin-sick souls. We come to church seeking hope for a cure of the situations that cause us much trauma, stress, and disconsolation during the week. We come to church needing a prescription that we can take home with us to make us act better and to provide a path to full recovery and wholeness of body, mind, and soul.

Now, as a doctor, my job is to diagnose your problem, prepare a treatment plan, consult with you, provide a regimen for you to follow, and then provide you with a prescription. Or I can assess your condition and then refer you to another authority for follow-up. Neither a doctor nor a nurse can make you well. And some medicines will make you feel worse before you get better. Every medicine has possible side-effects. Yet, too many of us will take those prescriptions, hoping for a magic and an instant cure, when the reality is that without a change in our lifestyle, without our full cooperation, and without taking all of the prescribed medicines we will never, ever get well.

Most of us will get our prescriptions filled, and then we begin this list of complaints: "Oh, this medicine is too bitter." "This medicine is too expensive." "This medicine makes me feel dizzy." "I started feeling better, so I stopped taking that medicine." All of these are our familiar excuses for not doing what we are supposed to do after the doctor has examined, diagnosed, and prescribed a regimen for us. Yet we want to blame the doctor because we don't get well.

Too many of us come to the church sick and go home feeling worse. Too many of us come to church and discover that there is no balm in Gilead. Too many of us come to church and there is no triage done by the healing team, comprised of the pastors and the musicians, to figure out just what it is that we need to make us well. So we have to seek better, more effective methods to discern the spirits that we face day after day, week after week.

It's always good to read, hear, learn, to be challenged to stretch and grow. Now it's time to deal with the realities of our lives. Let's do a quick and fool-proof discernment method with a brief survey: 1) if you have lost a child to death, please stop now and take a moment to regroup and to pray. 2) If you have lost a spouse to death, please take a moment to stop now, regroup, and pray. 3) If you have lost your job, been downsized on your job, or had to take a lower paying job, please stop now, take a moment to regroup, and pray. 4) If you have had a child in the court or prison system, or if you have experienced a breakup with your significant other or have been divorced this year, please take a moment to stop now, regroup, and pray. 5) If you have been diagnosed with diabetes, high cholesterol, high blood pressure, cancer, or heart disease, please take a moment to stop, regroup, and pray. 6) If for any reason you have had to physically move (relocate) this year, please stop now and take a moment to regroup and to pray.

These are the hurting spirits who come to visit each one of us. These are the haunting spirits that depress us, bow us down, and have us wanting to die! For these six stressful situations happen to all of us. There is no way around them. We cannot run away from them. We can't escape their coming to claim time in our home. These are situations that happen to all people, churched people and unchurched people alike, it makes no difference. For we are the stressed people and sick people who come to worship, seeking some sort of help, intervention, and deliverance, week after week.

The six stressful issues that I have listed and that we have faced cause the most stress in our lives. The world has taught us to try and to make it on our own. We try to fool ourselves and talk about the fact that we come from a strong people. Yet the reality is that hurt hurts and life changes wear at your spirit. Paul calls us to not try and get comfortable with the world's culture. As people of God, we are called to "test the spirits" by the Spirit to see if they are from God (1 John 4:1). Plan your life, being fully aware that these are incidents that you can weather. Be fully aware that these incidents happen to all of the people in your congregation. The Sovereign God has given us the ability to pray, to still our spirits through scripture reading and meditation, to allow soothing music to speak to us, for us, and about us, and to allow the healing process to begin.

As we know, the Pauline Epistles are concerned with the family of God. They deal with the intrachurch conflict that is pitting people against one another. The author of the book of 1 John addresses the church as "my dear children" or "beloved," terms of endearment and intimacy, wanting them to remember that they are connected through the blood of Jesus as sisters and brothers. The centrality of family is expressed in the ethical demand that we must love one another. Belief in the full humanity of Jesus is tied to the community's emphasis on love. For God is love.

When it comes to our worship, everything that we do must be based in the love of God for one another. The sharing of love is the mark of our being in the family of Jesus Christ. For those who love God must also love, be concerned about, and reach out to care for their siblings (1 John 4:21). So John the Elder essentially says, "Test the spirits. Discern the spirits. Watch the spirits. Be on guard for the spirits. Be alert to the spirits. And try them all against the Holy Spirit's love test."

We each have a human spirit; we call it our personality. Our human spirit can get in the way. Then there is the spirit of evil that is alive in the world. It too dwells in us, among us, and between us. Finally, there is God's Holy Spirit, who calls forth the agape love of God from us, in spite of us. As we work together, being the body of Christ, aware of all the various spirits that will be present in our house, at our job, in the grocery and department stores, as well as in the house of prayer on Sunday mornings, we have to first of all test our own spirit! And we have to ask ourselves, "Where is the love?"

We have to be prepared to *listen* to the soft and gentle voice of the Holy Spirit. We have to be prepared to *seek counsel* from others. We need each other to test and to try the spirits at work among us. We need to *shed our ego needs* as we test and try the spirits. God is all about the healing of sick people.

Our individual statement of purpose as we move out into our day ought to be: "All for God. Nothing less. Nothing else." If the words of our mouth do not point the people to God, it must be deleted from our repertoire. If the ways that we behave, with all of our activities, do not address the pain in our midst, point people to wholeness in God, and provide them with healing balm, it must not be on our schedule. Test the spirits by the Spirit and see if they are from God.

Discernment is a spiritual gift, my friends. Discernment is a community gift. Discernment is the ability to see the unseen, to look past the physical, and to hear and to acknowledge the voice of the Holy Spirit, who will provide us with direction. Discernment is the pastoral care factor of ministry. We go to classes in order to learn the academic pieces of our tasks; we can attend seminars and workshops to pick up new education. But discernment is about those interior, unspoken needs that you and I are charged to reach so that healing might begin.

Levites, ministers of music, choir directors, musicians, choir members, Sunday school teachers, ushers, and pastors, are jointly called to be doctors within and outside of the household of faith; and we are to remember that we, too, are the sin-sick.

A master teacher was asked by his student, "How will I know the Savior when I go down to the leprosy colony? I know that the Savior is always present among the sick." The master teacher replied, "All of the other lepers will take off all of their bandages to change their wounds at the same time. The Savior will take his off one at a time, in case he has to stop and help out another."

We are each part of God's healing team. Our job is to see the sin that is causing the sickness in us and among us and to address it by its proper name, sin. We are to confess our own sins and be freed of them. We are to consult with the sin-sick in love, encouraging them to confess and to repent. We are to encourage the sin-sick with hope. We are to testify to others of our own deliverance as a means of sharing what God has done in our lives. And we are to name their remedy as a return to a relationship with God. We are to provide them with the prescription that is salvation through Jesus Christ. Then, we are to refer them to the power of the Holy Spirit, who is the specialist. "All for God. Nothing less. Nothing else." "Beloved, do not conform any longer to the pattern of this world, but be transformed by the renewing of your mind."

Beloved's Personal Journey

The apostle Paul was a kind man, but one who did not bite his tongue or refrain from giving people difficult truth. He wanted everyone to know that there was the wrath of God to deal with when we fail to comply with the standards set by God. Many church folks don't like to talk about God's wrath, judgment, and condemnation of our sin. Paul was filled with the gift of spiritual discernment. He saw through flimsy excuses, evil people, and ungodly circumstances. The gift of spiritual discernment is yet alive, well, and practiced within the church.

1. When did you first realize that there was illness, sickness, and even evil within the local church?

2. If the Holy Spirit did a diagnostic of your spirituality, what area of your life would need immediate medical attention?

3. How did you recognize that, although you were "saved," there were yet interior wounds that required attention?

4. Describe the gift of spiritual discernment in your own language.

5. Name two or three personal friends who have the gift of spiritual discernment.

6. When was the last time you realized that something "funny" was going on or being said?

7. Write in your own words your goal of paying closer attention to the spiritual gift of discernment in your life.

3

WHO IS THE HOLY SPIRIT?

Do not behave as if you are doing God a favor!
God is the gift giver!

L. H.

Beloved, by the grace given me, I say to every one of you:
Do not think of yourself more highly than you ought, but rather
think of yourself with sober judgment, in accordance with the
measure of faith God has given you.

Romans 12:3 NIV

AT THE START OF THE LAST CENTURY, YEARS AGO, WHEN THINGS were different, there was a period when candles were in vogue and electricity was an infant. It required much work, money, and risk-taking ability to even consider the new way of living without candles. Many were eligible. Few were willing to be risk takers. Yet in one city there was this very wealthy and very frugal woman. Everyone knew her and was shocked when the word went forth that she was going to have electricity installed. The engineers arrived. Holes were dug. Poles were sunk into the ground and wires were strung to her home. Finally, the time came and the switches were thrown. She had electric lights.

The next month the meter reader came. The meter showed very little usage of electricity. He knocked on the door to inquire about any problems. When the home owner answered the door, the meter reader asked his pertinent question: "How are things going with your new electricity?" She responded, "Everything is fine." He asked, "Are you sure you know how to use the service we installed?" She replied, "Everything is fine." So, he pressed a bit harder. "Ma'am, the meter shows that you have used your electric service very little. I just need to know why." The kindly faced older woman looked at the concerned young man. Then she said, "I wait until just before dark. Then, I turn on the lights until I can see how to light my candles. I don't need your service for more than that."

I can join with you and laugh at this foolish woman until I think about myself in our very contemporary and technological lifestyle. I have bought two computers in the past five years. Both of them have massive hard drives, one has CD, DVD, telecamera, and video conferencing capability. Both computers will keep my calendar, update my checking and savings accounts, do spreadsheets, and allow me to converse with the whole wide world. We have a color scanner, a color printer, a fax machine—the works. And, like the lady in the previous century, I am limited to using the word processing program to write sermons and books. Both the older woman and this "hip-hop" pastor are not utilizing all the resources placed at our disposal. She and I have both paid for the services that will make our lives more enjoyable and filled with less hassle. She and I have decided to use snippets out of the vast network before us.

This is also the story of God's people, called the church. We have before us the Trinity. We praise God, who is our Creator. We uplift Jesus Christ, who is our Redeemer. We have the gift of the Holy Spirit, who is our comforter, leader, guide and renewer of life. Yet, most of us live without tapping into the power and availability of the Holy Spirit. When the Holy Spirit is not at work in your daily life, you are like the woman who was paying for electricity and using candles. You are like the pastor who has Internet capabilities and uses only the old electric typewriter portion of today's technology. For with your salvation, you have paid for all the resources that heaven has put within our reach. Yet, the reality is that most of us never stop to ask for the power of the Holy Spirit to be in charge of our lives.

We know *about* the Holy Spirit. We sing the Gloria Patri: "Glory be to the Father, and to the Son, and to the Holy Ghost." We give honor to the Holy Spirit. We sing the Doxology: "Praise God from whom all blessings flow. Praise God, all creatures here below. Praise Creator, Son, and Holy Ghost." But knowing about electricity, knowing about computers, and knowing about the powerful, indwelling presence of the Living God is different from utilizing the electricity, being able to navigate the Internet, and living life guided by the Holy Spirit. Paul introduces us to and wants us to become better acquainted with the Comforter, the Guide, the Gentle Prompter, and the Healer of wounded spirits, who is part of the Trinity and available to live inside each believer.

As Paul writes to the church at Ephesus, a group of gentiles who have accepted Jesus Christ as the way to God, he begins his pastoral epistle by reminding them in chapter 1, verses 4 and 5, that even though they were not born "worthy Jews," God had elected them, chosen them, and accepted them, through adoption as children. In verse 7 he reminds them that in Jesus Christ we have redemption, forgiveness, wisdom, and insight. It is given lavishly and freely. But look at verse 11, where there is the promise of an inheritance. When we heard and accepted the Word of God and believed Jesus Christ for salvation, we were given the seal of the Holy Spirit. The seal is the stamp of God's adoption and our membership within the body of Christ. The seal is the identifying mark that says we have dual citizenship, both in this world and throughout eternity.

What we know about God and what we do for God are often at odds with each other. Belief and behavior need to go hand in hand when the Holy Spirit is in leadership of our lives. There are fractures all over the place—fractures in our marriages, fractures in our relationships at work and in church, fractures in our bodies, spirits, and joints. The work of the Holy Spirit is to mend, to bring into reconciliation, and to heal the fractures among us. It is the work of the Holy Spirit to release the energy of healing among the people of God. We cannot do it by ourselves. We must be led, empowered, and motivated by the Holy Spirit. God has a long-range plan for the universe. Paul lets us in on the secret that the Holy Spirit is the healer of our fractured world.

The Holy Spirit is not an "it." The Holy Spirit is not a "he" or a "she." The Holy Spirit is the presence of God, alive, active and ministering in the world. The Holy Spirit has always been dispatched to touch, empower, and enable God's will to be done throughout history. The Holy Spirit is the Breath of God, who blew upon the chaos of eternity and brought the world's energy into order. God spoke. Christ agreed. And the Holy Spirit worked. The words "breath" and "wind" signify the movement of God both in the world and in our life. You can't see the wind. You can't predict the wind. You can't control or limit the wind. You can either work with its current or be blown away. In the same manner, you cannot "get" the Holy Spirit in the manner that our Pentecostal friends instruct us to do. All we can do is pray, submit, and allow the Holy Spirit to "get" us! And for this to happen we have to be willing to get self, ego and "I" out of the way!

Another name that we, as United Methodists, use for the Holy Spirit is Preeminent Grace, God's amazing Grace that is intervening, wooing, calling us when we have decided to turn away from God. I heard of a story the other day about a professional couple who had made the decision that they did not need God through church, worship, and community as they had been raised. But God gave them the gift of a baby girl. That baby girl went to preschool and heard other children talking about Jesus, singing Sunday school songs. It was the intervening Grace of God who had the child come and question her parents. Today they are all active in the work of ministry due to the Holy Spirit's movement through children.

Each of us has an intervening grace story. Someone prayed for each one of us until the time we made a decision for Christ and salvation. Confessing Christ as Savior is the work of the Holy Spirit in our lives. For "justifying" Grace is our act of repenting and God's act of erasing our histories before Christ, and treating us as if we were in right relationship all the time. God's promise is to "tread our sins underfoot, and hurl all our iniquities into the depths of the sea" (Micah 7:19, NIV). Just as we are, without one plea, we can come and find our homes in God. Yet, there is more.

There is "sanctifying" grace. There is the work of the Holy Spirit within us to make us more like Jesus than we have ever imagined we could become. Sanctifying grace is not about you jumping and shouting. Sanctifying grace is not about your receiving the gift of a new prayer language. Sanctifying grace is not about you having more spiritual gifts and more advanced spiritual knowledge than others. Sanctifying grace is the Holy Spirit at work in you to say "NO!" to sin and "YES!" to the will and the way of God. The Holy Spirit comes to lead us, to guide us, and to heal us so that we can become imitators of Jesus Christ in all the world. Jesus said to the disciples before the day of his ascension, "It is expedient for you that I go away; for if I do not go away, the Comforter will not come unto you. But if I depart, I will send the Holy Spirit unto you" (John 16:7 KJV). This is the promise of promises. This is the source of all our help. This is the paraclete, the one sent not only to walk beside us, but to live in and through us as the agency of God.

The Holy Spirit is our teacher. John 15:26 (NIV) says, "When the Comforter is come, whom I will send unto you . . . , even the Spirit of truth, . . . the Holy Spirit will testify of me." It is the role of the Holy Spirit to give witness in our spirit when the spoken word is that which comes from Jesus Christ. John says in chapter 14:26, "The Comforter, the Holy Spirit, whom God will send in my name, will teach you all things and will remind you of everything I have said to you." The Holy Spirit is our guide. For John 16:12–14 (NKJV) declares, "I still have many things to say to you, but you cannot bear them now. However, when . . . the Spirit of Truth has come, the Spirit will guide you into all truth." The Holy Spirit is the leader of the church of God. For Romans 8:14 (NKJV) declares, "For as many as are led by the Spirit of God, these are the sons and daughters of God." The Holy Spirit is our helper. Romans 8:26

(NKJV) declares that "the Spirit also helps us with our weaknesses. For we do not know what we should pray for as we ought, but the Spirit makes intercession for us with groanings which cannot be uttered."

Finally, the Holy Spirit is our own, personal indwelling power pack. John 14:16–17 reminds us that Jesus promised us the Holy Spirit, "whom the world cannot receive," because the world cannot see or know the presence of God. You, however, know the presence of the Holy Spirit, for the Holy Spirit has come to dwell with you and to live within you.

Without the Holy Spirit at work in us, with us, through us, and even in spite of us, we are simply people who are living with full access to electricity but operating with the dimness of candles. Without the Holy Spirit leading our lives, witnessing through us and doing the healing in the name of the Christ, we are simply people using old fashioned typewriters while new computer technology sits idle and unused. Jesus knew how afraid the disciples were. So when he rose from the grave and came to find them, hiding out in the Upper Room, he walked in and bid them "peace" and then breathed on them the Holy Spirit. These scared cowards became the church.

It's our turn. Let's pray the prayer of asking the Holy Spirit to come and live within us.

For the Holy Spirit wants to be asked to come and take charge. It's all about our submitting to the Healer of Broken Hearts, the Healer of Ruptured Relationships, the Healer of Wounded Spirits, who wants to touch us, fill us, empower us, and make us electrifying witnesses and powerful healers in all the world that we touch.

The song is a prayer and the prayer is a song: "Breathe on me Breath of God. Fill me with life anew. That I may love what thou would love and do what thou would do!"[1]

"Beloved, by the grace given me, I say to every one of you: Do not think of yourself more highly than you ought, but rather think of yourself with sober judgment, in accordance with the measure of faith God has given you."

Beloved's Personal Journal

We cannot believe all that we see, nor all that we hear. And we cannot believe all that we feel! The apostle Paul warns the people not to give in to the false pride of arrogance that seems to embrace too many church folks! For some reason, when we join church, get some seniority, and hold a few offices, there is a tendency to begin to feel more superior than others, both in and out of the church. Paul wants every Christian to be what God has called each to be, no more and, certainly, no less than what God has divinely designed.

1. Write down three of your best personal attributes.

2. Write down three of your worst personal attributes.

3. Write down how your best friend would describe you.

4. Write down what your worst enemy would say about you.

5. What is your goal for asking the Holy Spirit to work in and on you?

4

DO YOU REMEMBER?

*Our physical bodies are comprised
of many different functioning parts.*

L. H.

*Beloved, just as each of us has one body
with many members, . . . these members do not
all have the same function.*

Romans 12:4 NIV

DO YOU REMEMBER? THIS QUESTION STARTS MINDS TO SWIRLING, thoughts get to clicking, and the brain begins to engage in reflections of yesterday.

Do you remember? This is a time to pause and recall moments lived, experiences gone by, and occasions that have already happened.

Do you remember? Sometimes joy is relived. Sometimes pain is recalled. Sometimes a smile comes to your face. At other times the tears begin to roll. Sometimes places are visited. Sometimes old scenes begin to flash. At other times individuals appear available to be encountered afresh and anew. For many people and experiences come into our lives and then leave. They have made an imprint upon us. Many of them are worth our remembering.

Do you remember? Memory is a gift. Memory is a blessing. Memory is a requirement for our growth, development, and educational formation. Memory is the building block upon which we build one life experience, which carries us to the next one. We learn the alphabet in order to learn how to read. We learn to count in order to learn how to do complicated math. Like a computer, the storage files of our mind hold what we know and connect it to our new experiences. Do you remember?

We often gather in community to ask the question again. We gather at funerals and at memorials to give thanks for yesterday's memories, today's opportunities, and tomorrow's hope. We gather with family and friends in reunions, to take deliberate time to remember. We remember loved ones. We remember their significance in our lives. We remember the joy they brought. We remember the stunts they pulled, the personalities they shared, the pain they brought as well as the life lessons taught. In our denomination, on All Saints Sunday, we sing a chime, light a candle, call out their names, and remember.

Do you remember that Jesus, our Sovereign and Savior, commanded that we stop and remember? As the song "Lord, I Lift Your Name on High" says, "You came from heaven to earth to show us the way; from the earth to the cross, my debt to pay; from the cross to the grave, from the grave to the sky."[1] As we lift his name on high, we remember.

We remember his moving into our skin. We remember his living in our neighborhood. We remember his walking in our shoes. We remember his eating at our tables. We remember his healing our bodies, raising our dead, giving sight to our blind, and shedding our tears.

We remember him teaching us. We remember his feeding us. We remember his washing our feet. We remember him telling us to "go and sin no more." We remember him calling our children to him. We remember him sending us back out to fish in deeper waters. We remember him calling us by name as we haunted our own empty places, searching for one who would love us, accept us as we were, and provide purpose and direction for our lives.

We remember the wonderful and vulnerable personality of Jesus. We remember the tender teaching moments of Jesus. We remember the touching stories of Jesus. We remember the various ways he drew people to him. We love to remember the good times. Jesus, however, commanded that we both remember and celebrate his full life, not simply what we feel are pleasant and precious memories. "Remember me," says Jesus. "Remember me."

Do you remember the context of this command? It was after thirty-three years of living in poverty with people who thought he was too big for his britches! It was after three and a half years of healing, teaching, and feeding throughout little ghetto areas. It was after being misunderstood, not accepted, and doubted that Jesus told those closest to him, "Don't forget me. Remember me."

Do you remember the setting of this command? Jesus had been the hero of a Palm Sunday parade. The branches had been waved, hosannas had been cheered, the excitement had been high, but that high moment didn't last. Betrayal was in the air. Pain was on the horizon. Intense intercession with pleading and sweating was just ahead. A trial was going to be held. Lies were going to be told. And a cross was in his future. He wanted those closest to him to recall the full picture. He didn't want them left with only selective memory.

So Jesus put on an apron and knelt down, like their servant, to wash their feet. Jesus became the cook, preparing a meal from his own body and blood. Then Jesus served his friends and said, "Remember me." Remember my life. Remember my ministry. Remember my love. Remember my servanthood. Remember my highs. Remember my lows. Remember my joys. Remember my pain. Remember my celebrations. Remember my tears. Remember my exploits. Remember my struggles. Remember my life. Remember my death. With all the complexities of our time together, remember me.

Do you remember? He took bread and broke it. It was a sign, a symbol, and a token of his body broken for us. He told them to take and eat the broken pieces of life and to remember that we are each part of the whole body of Christ. He took the wine, a sign, a symbol, and a token of his life's blood, poured out and shed for the remission of our sin. And he told them to drink it as we remember that our salvation cost him his life. And he summed it all up by saying that he would not eat with them again until that heavenly banquet on the other side of Calvary's cross.

Do you remember? Calvary and death were not the end. Calvary, death, and a borrowed tomb were not the final words. Calvary, death, sin, and hell could not prevent the resurrection. For Jesus Christ got up! Jesus Christ arose, victorious over every obstacle of our human lives. Nothing can separate us from this triumphant love of God for us in Christ Jesus, for we are Easter people! Rising is our song of constant praise!

So, do you remember? The apostle Paul helps us to remember the story of our common faith as he writes and instructs. Do you remember? He calls us to take the time to pause, in the midst of business and busy-ness, to bring back to our collective memories the lives, the witness and the ministries of those in our beloved community who now await us on the other side of death and the grave.

Do you remember? As we call their names they answer in our hearts. They are simply our balcony saints. They are our cheerleading section. They are the communion of the faith-filled, waiting to see how well we will remember the gifts of their lives.

The scripts of these important people in our human existence have now been complete. The charge given unto their hands is done. The purpose for which they were born has been fulfilled. And yet, they live. They live on in our memories. We see their smiles. We hear their voices. Flashes, glimpses, and sudden appearances of them occur over and over again, for we are blessed with the gift of memory, which is a mini-resurrection story.

This very day, although gone from our visual sight, each one is present to us, for they imparted blessings and invested in our lives. This day, wherever we are located, even as the grief wells and the tears roll, they stand tall in us. This day, they might be absent from us bodily and present with God, but they are also with us, by the powerful gift of memory. Because they played their part, carried out their function, and fulfilled their divine purpose upon the earth, we celebrate their lives, applaud their achievements, and say like the heavenly host did upon their arrival into eternity, "Well done, good and faithful servants." Do you remember?

"Beloved, just as each of us has one body with many members, all of our members do not have the same function."

Beloved's Personal Journal

Relationships are essential to Christian community. The apostle Paul goes to great length to establish how Jesus Christ has made the way possible for sinful humans to be united in a new relationship with God, through the atoning work of Calvary. He then presses on to help new Christians to be willing to do the more difficult work of being in good, healthy, and wholesome relationships with one another. The local church environment and the assembly of believers were essential to the ministry. Each one was given gifts to be used for the up-building of the body. Each one had an important, even essential role to carry out as they all invested into each other's lives. All members had different, diverse and distinct purposes to carry out, and as they worked together the multitude of ministry opportunities had a huge impact, one on the other.

1. Out of your childhood congregation, whom do you best remember?
2. What important personality in the local congregation had the most impact upon you?
3. How did they exhibit their spiritual gifts?
4. When did you realize that this person had chosen to invest in your life?
5. What of this individual do you hope to invest in another person's life?
6. Write down three things that you want people to remember about you.

5

GIFT WRAPPED

The body of Christ is one unit,
and all of us have a part to play in it.

L. H.

Beloved, we who are in Christ form one body,
and each member belongs to all the others.

Romans 12:5 NIV

HISTORY IS DEFINED BY CERTAIN NOTICEABLE EVENTS. HISTORY is recorded because of the deeds that are done and remembered by people who were touched. Incidents become history because somebody did something that caused others to pause and take notice of the changes that occurred afterwards. History is made most often by people who are not prepared to do the extraordinary.

More than forty-five years ago Mrs. Rosa Parks made history. A short, petite African American seamstress changed the course of events in this country by sitting where no black person had ever sat before. Mrs. Parks was coming from work, tired. On that particular day she sat in the first available seat of a Montgomery, Alabama, bus. When asked to move so a white person could have her seat, she refused. By her refusal to move, the system of segregation, Jim Crow and unequal treatment began to slowly unravel, unwind, and change.

Her actions were not strategized or planned. Her need to take the first available seat to rest her tired body was not the result of any political scheme to wreak havoc with the normal and accustomed way of life in America. But on that day Mrs. Parks manifested the divine image of God within her. That small epiphany became history. It was the work of the Holy Spirit that called the mother of the civil rights struggle to use her spiritual gifts of faith in God, courage, and boldness in the Holy Spirit to remain seated even after being cursed, sworn at, vilified, and eventually arrested. Because she dared to sit and remain seated more than forty-five years ago, things became different. History was made.

We are well aware that history was also made by Dr. Martin Luther King Jr., who was born during the season of Epiphany, when we begin to more fully discover the Christ is in our midst. Epiphany is the season of our perceiving, discovering, and recognizing the Holy One among us. Epiphany is the time when our fears and our prejudices, which prevent us from having an authentic relationship with the Christ, are unmasked, shattered, and dispelled. Epiphany is the occasion when we more fully comprehend that we are each called to encounter and recognize the sacred and the divine. During the season of epiphany we come to better appreciate that the sacred, the divine, is already enfolded, wrapped up, and encased within each of us called by the name of the Son of God. Just as the magi brought their treasures to the Christ child, in the season of Epiphany each of us is to discover, develop, and deploy the gift that we are. For you are the gift! And the spiritual gifts of God are already within you.

Spiritual gifts are not delivered by Federal Express, Parcel Post, or the U.S. Postal Service. Spiritual gifts are deposited within us by the work of the Holy Spirit before our birth.

1 Corinthians 12:11 plainly states that it is the role of the Holy Spirit to assign spiritual gifts. Verse 7 tells us that none of us are left out of the assignment pool. This verse goes on to further detail that our gifts are given for the benefit of the whole church. "To each one the manifestation of the Spirit is given for the common good" (NIV). And the gifts are different, assorted, unalike, not the same, a Heinz 57 variety, if you will, in order that

we can work together and celebrate our common movement toward being the church. We don't all do it the same. God loves variety. Variety is the spice of life. And, in the variety of our assorted gifts, it is the same God who activates them all.

Paul cautions us not to miss God because of blindness and misinformation. We need to always be on the alert for a sighting of the Holy One. Remember when Jesus and the growing group of disciples followed his mother to a friend's wedding? Jesus, like Rosa Parks more than forty-five years ago, manifested the gift of miracle working power. The people were poor and the wine ran out. Mary turned to Jesus and informed him of the lack of wine. For what is a wedding where the wine, which brings joy, is lacking? Marriage and joy are intertwined. Marriage is a sacred coupling between God and the church. And the Holy Spirit's ministry among us is the joy of our salvation. What happens when the joy is gone? Like Mary, we need turn to Jesus. However, Jesus looked at his mother and asked what this lack of joy-giving wine had to do with him. Mary got silent, refusing to argue with her son, the Messiah. But she turned to the servants and informed them to "do whatever he tells you." This is the role of the church, to do whatever Jesus tells us. So the servants took heed and followed her instructions. For Mary knew that the fullness of God was wrapped up in Jesus. Jesus was the gift, sitting in the audience, at an ordinary event, waiting for his glass of wine!

The Bible says that turning the water into wine was the first of his signs. It was another epiphany and a small glimpse of the appearance of God, who said that even the poor people of Cana in Galilee deserved the excellent wine of joy! When the wine was tasted by the steward and its robust flavor discovered, the disciples, the followers, the ones who were tagging along for the ride, became true believers. At an unexpected occasion, they saw for themselves that the gift of God was wrapped in the human flesh of Jesus.

Our spiritual journey so reflects the pages of Holy Scripture. We, too, have a marriage between ourselves and Jesus Christ. For we, the church, are the bride of Christ. A marriage is not an easy relationship. It has both highs and lows. A marriage goes through seasons. And, yes, there is the season of wondering what happened to the initial love. Strong wills, diverse opinions, and different life seasons will cause us to ponder whether the passion and momentum once enjoyed can be recovered and rekindled. So the season of Epiphany comes with a loud shout of "Yes!" For if we take our empty jars of clay, fill them to the brim with the waters of hope, prayer, daily devotion, persistence, and commitment to the marriage, we find that when the youthful, lustful attracting love is gone, a deeper, more fulfilling and lasting love is discovered. Then we really have a marriage. However, joy is available only after we are each willing to "Do what Jesus says."

You are the gift! Say it with me, " I am the gift. All I need is already within me." Our spiritual gifts too often lie dormant and not activated for service. Yet it is the same God who loves us and assigned us our destiny in life who calls each of us to discover, develop, and deploy our spiritual gift, which is always an epiphany event.

If you already know your spiritual gift, name it, operate in it, and share it in conversation openly and with deliberation these next weeks. For the reality is that the use of our spiritual gift is our act of love back to God. It is the opening of our treasure chest before the our sovereign God. And it is only in loving service, nurturing each other and the world, that we discover that the more love we give away, the more love we receive. God's amazing love brings the wine of joy to the marriage between us and our Christ!

Beloved's Personal Journal

Unity was a key component of the emerging church as folks came together and sought to become "family," the body of Christ. The apostle Paul realized that if the church was to impact, influence, and transform the world, each one had bring to his or her spiritual gifts into operation. The church is built upon the principle that one person can add to the mix, but a team of people, working in unity, multiplies the efforts and maximizes outcomes.

Uniformity was not Paul's aim or goal. He realized that God wanted vitality and versatility in the body of Christ, not sameness! Everyone has and is a gift!

1. Where do you "fit" within the body of Christ?

2. What is the "gift" that you offer to Christ?

3. How did you come to recognize that you were gifted?

4. Who, in your local church, affirmed your spiritual gifts?

5. How does your local congregation celebrate its diversity?

6

STIR UP THE GIFTS

*All of us have meaning, purpose, and function
within the body of Christ. We must work together for the
body to be excellently formed and marvelously fashioned
in the way God has designed.*

L. H.

*Beloved, we have different [spiritual] gifts,
according to the grace [that God has] given to each of us.
If your gift is prophesying, then prophesy in
accordance with your faith.*

Romans 12:6 TNIV

ONCE UPON A TIME THERE WAS THIS WOMAN WHO HAD amassed a great fortune with her spouse. She and he had built a great newspaper company over the years. They had three children, all of whom they had reared and educated and who lived fairly lavishly off what their parents had accomplished. The man died, and the woman felt that surely one of her children would offer to come and to work with her. But the three children, an oldest son, a spoiled oldest daughter, and a baby girl, continued with their own lives. The woman had a trusted companion who had been with the paper as long as she and her spouse had. She felt that he would be the one to manage the paper when her twilight came. That twilight came sooner than she expected when her kidneys began to fail.

The name of the novel that tells this story is *When Twilight Comes* by Gwynne Forster.[1] Gwen writes to cause women my age to pause and consider who will benefit from my hard and diligent labors after I'm gone. I have had to work hard, study long, burn the midnight oil, keep my face to the sky, and forsake many desired material things in order to pay for education, books, and school loans, while raising children at the same time. Who will I invest my life into as I face death?

When the woman in the story decides that she will not undergo the stress of dialysis three times a week and chooses to die a natural death, she insists that one of her three children step up to the plate and come to learn the news business. In a complex series of twists and turns, the two older siblings decide to keep doing what they have chosen to do in life. The youngest sibling, a college professor, is up for tenure in her career, and yet she is the one who steps up to assist their mother. It's fine with the older two, until . . . until they learn that their mother is bequeathing, willing, and leaving the entire industry in the hands of the youngest child.

Like many of us in the church, the two oldest siblings did not want to work for the money they thought was rightfully theirs. The two oldest siblings felt that it was theirs by birthright. The two oldest siblings had no quarrel with the youngest sibling leaving her tenured position, changing her lifestyle, and forsaking her office, acquaintances, and peers to start all over again. The two oldest siblings were not willing to work with their mother, not willing to give up their independence, not willing to go the extra mile for what they felt simply belonged to them. They didn't want the headaches, didn't want the pressures, and didn't want the depression that comes with starting over, following the leader, and taking orders from the one who knows the way!

But when twilight came, the mother made some new decisions. When twilight came, the mother decided that the one who was willing to transfer her loyalty, bridge her skill-sets, offer her gifts, become part of a new team, and follow the mother's orders would be the one who earned her legacy. It's quite a story. It's a thinking parents' story. It reminded me of the apostle Paul and a young preacher named Timothy.

Paul was a parent figure and a mentor to young Timothy. Paul was the officiant at Timothy's ordination service. Paul was well acquainted with young Timothy's mother and grandmother, Lois and Eunice. Paul had stayed at their home. Timothy had traveled and learned how to do missionary and evangelistic work with Paul.

Like that mother with the newspaper business, Paul had a legacy that he wanted to leave behind. Paul had spent years laboring with gentiles, establishing congregations, teaching, preaching, uplifting, evangelizing, admonishing, and pastoring God's crazy people. Paul realized that his neck would soon be on the line. And, like any of us, when the twilight of our years begins to roll around, Paul was wrestling with the issue of depression.

Depression! Depression! Depression: a word that we don't like to deal with in the church. Depression: anger at something that we turn into ourselves. Depression: fear that our best has not been good enough, that we have not measured up and that what we have done will die with us! Depression: a demonic thorn in the flesh of every child of God who dares to serve faithfully.

So, as Paul lay in a Roman prison, knowing that twilight was coming, that the end of the journey of many years was coming to an ugly end, he wanted to see who would take up his mantle and do the job to the best of his ability. So Paul decided to write this, his last letter, to young Timothy—who was also warring with the demon of depression!

Paul was old and scared. Timothy was young and scared. For depression, defeat, despair, and disillusionment have no respect of persons. Every child of God is a very fine target for demonic attacks. We live in a world where self-help is a by-product of our culture. Want to learn new technology? Buy a self-help book. Want to learn how to prepare gourmet meals? Buy a self-help cookbook. Want to learn to better manage your financial affairs? Buy a self-help book. Want to learn all that there is to know about a subject? Google it, search for it on the Internet, and print it out or save it to your hard drive. But when all of our self-help methods don't work, we feel defeated; we are filled with despair and disillusionment sets in and may turn into full-blown depression.

Paul was depressed but Paul was not down for the count. Paul realized that he had almost finished his course and that he needed to pass the baton on to another for the next section of the journey. So Paul wrote to tell Timothy how he, Paul, had kept going, kept persevering, kept pushing ahead in the war with evil. He said to Timothy, "Young Brother, stir up the gifts that are in you."

To stir up the gifts means that, first of all, Timothy had to know what spiritual gifts he had within him, by the laying on of hands and with the indwelling of the Holy Spirit in his life. Saints of the Most High God, we are not members of the church of self-help! I have come to announce that we don't belong to the "I can have it my way church," either. It might be bad news to many of you, but we don't have membership in the church of "I just want to see you smile!" We all belong to the church of the Living God. Jesus lived, died, and rose again to save us. Then Jesus sent back the power of the Holy Spirit to be received by each one of us so the Holy Spirit might lead us, guide us, inspire us, gift us, develop us, and deploy us within the body of Christ, everywhere we are needed, across the world.

Paul knew that Timothy was gifted as a pastor-teacher, an evangelist and an encourager of God's people. Paul had seen these gifts at work in Timothy. The Holy Spirit had Paul lay hands on Timothy to allow the infilling of this young man with power to battle the depression that hits all workers in God's realm. Stir up the gifts means to fan the dying embers that are lying within our spirits. Stir up the gifts means to go back to the place where we first met God, first had our love experience of God, and first discovered that, despite our mess, regardless of our mess-ups, and in spite of our messed-up backgrounds, God wanted to use us in service.

The Greek word for "stir" is a metaphor for fanning the flames of a dying fire. The reason for Christian revivals on an annual basis is that we all tend to get run down in ministry. We all get weary in our well-doing of ministry. We all get tired of God's crazy people in Christian ministry. Too many of us feel like perhaps the best thing that we can do is try to retire early, find another position, or simply throw in the towel. But revival is the time when the Holy Spirit comes to fan the dying flames within our spirits! Revival comes to give us another log to burn, another rich piece of the Word to inspire us, and another touch of the Divine Power that we might be renewed, re-adjusted, and revived to go back out and start all over again! So stir up the gifts that are in you! Don't allow your fire to go out!

Doesn't it seem strange to you that Paul didn't write some nice, pretty words to offer comfort to Timothy, who had been crying at their last meeting? Wouldn't you anticipate some sweet, enchanting, and endearing sentiments to be expressed, as this just might be the very last time that these two dear friends would communicate?

What I leaned from Paul in this passage of scripture is that, in order to be effective as we pass on the baton to another on the journey, we cannot always be nice in our communication. We cannot always be politically correct as we pass on God's orders. We cannot always be gentle and kind as we say, "Thus says God." God often demands our being abrupt, abrasive, and seemingly downright mean or even rude in order to keep people in line with their missions and their destinies! Nice words would not have motivated Timothy. Kind, easy sentiments would not have inspired him to stand up to the people he was charged to oversee as pastor. Political correctness would not have put the necessary message straight in Timothy's face. But the direct, harsh words "Stir up the gifts" made sense to Timothy, and they make sense to me and to you!

Timothy was between a rock and a hard place. His mentor was in jail. He had a group of recalcitrant church folks to deal with. He was young. And it's obvious that he was frightened of what lay ahead. Paul knew all of this. Paul was cognizant of this minister's fear of failure. Yet, Paul recognized that Timothy had been selected by God to pick up his baton and to run the race before him.

Now, the questions before Timothy were: Who wants a role model that is locked up in jail? Who wants to take on a job where the benefits are not in tangible stuff, material goods, nor earned in real time? Who wants to wrestle with empty pews, drastically unmet budgets, fighting choirs who want new robes but who cannot sing, along with an archaic bureaucracy in Jerusalem that is wholly out of touch and stuck in yesterday and the way we've always done things? Who wants to do the same old neighborhood canvass, the same old stewardship campaign, and the same old, typically not-working, not-effective week-long summer Vacation Bible School? Who wants to be lied about, talked about, not given a raise, not given respect, but blamed for everything that goes wrong, year, after year, after year? Who?

Paul was smart enough to know that the answer then was not Timothy and it's not any "Timothy" or "Linda" nowadays, either. So to set the record straight and get young Timothy back in line with the program, Paul took his pen in hand while in jail, and wrote, in his very last letter, "Stir up the gifts!"

Most of us try and exist with our weekly Sunday morning religious "fix." People of God, we cannot make it as effective Christians with a once-a-week shot in the Spirit! Our relationship with God is based on a loving, intimate, and moment-by-moment walk with the Holy Spirit leading and guiding our way. Where too many of us "new Christians" fail is in the area of asking the Holy Spirit to take control of our lives, our steps, and our way, each and every minute of the day. We cannot help ourselves! We cannot keep ourselves! And we cannot practice, steal, or imitate the gifts of the Holy Spirit for very long on our own!

God gives us our gifts specifically for the roles we are to play in the world. We somehow discover our spiritual gifts within Christian community. After we know what the role is that God has designed for us to play in this holy realm, then we can develop our spiritual gifts. Finally, it's role of the Holy Spirit to help us to then deploy our spiritual gifts in effective ways.

The church of the Living God has always been under attack! Jesus Christ was a revolutionary! His followers were honestly out of the box! Jesus had strange taste in company: fishermen, women with bad reputations who did not know their places, little snotty-nosed children, as well as foreigners and known sinners! Paul knew that he was no goodie-two-shoes. Timothy was young, whiney, and a crybaby. Yet, this assorted group of folks, who continued to hang with the Jesus Way, have caught our attention and brought us into being followers by way of their spiritual gifts.

I enjoy watching Joel Osteen. His practical, day-to-day principles as outlined in *Your Best Life Now*, a good self-help book, are good ones. I admire Rick Warren and will be ever so glad when my publisher can sell over fifteen million copies of any book that I write. So, I salute him and *The Purpose-Driven Life*.[2] Neither one of these books, however, attacks the sin problem at the core of our being. Neither one gives us insight into the need for the Holy Spirit to be at work in us, on us, through us, and in spite of us if we want to be successful as born-again Christians in a world that is so filled with deceit. Both books tend to help us feel that we can make it happen through a positive mindset, good intentions, and their self-help suggestions. It won't work!

We cannot make it with our little church membership, denominational ties, organizational affiliations, officer nominations, or elevated positions. None of these will get us into heaven and eternal life! They are good things to possess. They are good to do, but they won't keep us saved! Nor will they make us effective. For it requires the power of the living, guiding, directing Holy Spirit to lead us in the ways that please God and allow the church of Jesus Christ to be bold.

My ministry is grounded in the very fact that without the infilling of the Holy Spirit we will have a difficult if not impossible time living effectively for Jesus Christ. My Pentecostal roots, despite education, illumination, and sophistication remain embedded in my soul, and I cannot make it without asking the Spirit of the Living God to fall fresh one me. For I will cut up in a New York minute if the Holy Spirit is not putting a curb on me! I will act out without regard for who it hurts if the Holy Spirit is not in charge of me! I just know what is required for me to live holy, and it's the power, the leading, and the direction of the Holy Spirit.

I went to high school with Lonnell Johnson, who is now an English professor at Oberlin College in Ohio. Lonnell was smart in high school, but now he has a PhD and is also an ordained minister. This makes him "super anointed and smart"! He shared a tape on the Holy Spirit with me. I appreciated his definitions about some of the functions of the Holy Spirit. He gave me permission to share them with you. His terms are in italics.

When the Holy Spirit is received, for the Holy Spirit is a gift, the Holy Spirit will come to take up residence in a clean temple. This means that as long as we remain clean and holy the Holy Spirit will do the work of assisting our lives. The Holy Spirit, however, cannot remain where sin resides! So, the Holy Spirit comes with *validation* that we are truly saved, clean, and born again.

The next function of the Holy Spirit is to give us an *impartation* of God's imprint on our lives. I am the Light wherever I am. God shines through me due to the impartation of the Holy Spirit at work in my life. This impartation causes us *separation* from the evil of our past and the world. We no longer care to do the same old things or to keep company with the old friends of our past. After our separation comes our *transformation*. Paul declares that we are transformed by the renewing of our mind. And that renewing and transforming agent is none other than the Holy Spirit, who comes to teach us all things that Jesus taught while on earth. With our transformation we get *activation*, and our evangelizing begins. "Go, into all the world . . . witness, convert, teach, catechize, baptize, and make new believers!" We have a strategy, a system, and a substance of power, the Holy Spirit!

Now, catch this one from the depths of Dr. Johnson: *Televisualization* is the direct result of our activation by the Holy Spirit! Televisualization is the ability to see dimensionally. We can "see" what's occurring in the present world, and we can "see" what it means spiritually as our citizenship is no longer of this world. In plain English, I'd call it discernment to know evil, wicked, and ugly stuff. For we are to try the Spirits by the Holy Spirit to see if they are of God!

From televisualization, we get *initiation* into a new family with a new name. Remember the old saints singing the spiritual, "I told Jesus it would be alright if he changed my name"?

With our initiation into the fellowship of believers, we incur an *obligation*. Many of us are members of sororities and fraternities where the rites of passage, the "secret orders," and the "crossing over the burning sands" are obligatory in order to belong. Our obligation as baptized, Spirit-filled believers is to live right according to biblical "orders," to support the church (family) with our tithes and offerings, to seek the lost (unsaved), and to spread the message of Jesus everywhere that we go! When we actually live within this realm, we move to *new revelation*.

When the Holy Spirit comes to live within us, God can trust us with new secret knowledge! We can know the "secrets," the mind of God. And we can be exposed to and even experience the height, depth, and length of God's love! "We do, however, speak a message of wisdom among the mature, but not the wisdom of this age or of the rulers of this age, who are coming to nothing. No, we speak of God's secret wisdom, a wisdom that has been hidden and that God destined for our glory before time began" (1 Cor. 2:6–7 NIV).

I really want to thank my "homeboy" for this powerful explanation of the Holy Spirit that is done with poetic excellence! Give a round of applause for my old Gary, Indiana, native, Rev. Dr. Lonnell Johnson!

Many of us have been "touched" by the power of the Holy Spirit at one time or another, but to be a bodacious Christian, we need to be filled with the Holy Spirit. This will allow the Holy Spirit to move from *visitation* to *habitation*! And we can create this atmosphere of habitation by simply inviting the Holy Spirit to "come in today, come in to stay. Come into my heart, O Lord Jesus!"[3] For when Jesus returned to heaven, with all power the Holy Spirit was released into the earthly realm to help us be as bold as needed for the living of these days!

As we help each other to cope with the pressures of our days, let's keep the praise song, the prayer song, and the prayer request upon our lips: "Spirit of the Living God, fall afresh on me. Spirit of the Living God, fall afresh on me. Melt me, mold me, fill me, use me. Spirit of the Living God, fall afresh on me."[4] Amen! Please remember me, for I'm singing this prayer as we journey too!

So, Beloved, "we have different spiritual gifts, according to the grace that God has given us." Stir them up and use them!

Beloved's Personal Journal

The grace (*charis*) of God, which brings to us salvation through our faith in God as evidenced in Jesus Christ, also offers to each believer spiritual gifts (*charismata*) that we are to utilize to make the body of Christ more effective. The apostle Paul knew that with our diverse gifts and our distinct personalities a great challenge lay ahead for the spreading church. He wanted the members to recognize that we are each different in the ways that we perform our roles and yet because we are "different" that does not mean that any of us are necessarily deficit because we do not do things the same way! This can make a fascinating mix of people who have the divine challenge to make the body function well together.

1. Every "normal" and "healthy" system will experience unease, unrest, and conflict due to the "differences" of both gifts and personalities. How was reconciliation achieved in your family of origin?

2. How is reconciliation achieved in your current family situation?

3. How is reconciliation achieved in your local congregation?

4. What spiritual gifts are "missing" in your local church?

5. Whom do you need to encourage to offer their gifts into service?

7

YOU MATTER IN LOVE

Do what God has chosen, called, and designed you to do!

L. H.

Beloved, if [your gift] is serving, then serve.
If it is teaching, then teach.

Romans 12:7 TNIV

No one touches people's lives exactly the way that YOU do! There are hurts only YOUR hugs can heal; problems that only YOUR advice can solve; stress that only YOUR kindness can ease. YOUR caring and insight are unmatched! And that trademark smile of YOURS—the one that comes from the heart—has all the power to get other people smiling again. Even YOUR worries make a difference, because they show people how deeply YOU care! The fact is, YOU make the world a better place! It's a simple truth: YOU don't have to be rich or famous to have an impact on the world. All YOU have to do is to be YOURSELF![1]

It's the matter of sharing God's love. You and I are it! What a wonderful thing to be able to share with you about the joy, the pleasure, the delight, and the awesome impact that you make upon those who are blessed to be in your presence. What a good thing to be able to remind you, of the blessed people who were before you and assisted you with your becoming who you are today! What a privilege to take this time to help you to spend a few minutes renaming those folks who invested in your life and caused you to become the individual who invests in the life of others today. So why not take it as a time to share a little love every day?

God knows YOU! God loves YOU! God has big plans for YOUR life! God is love. And by adoption, baptism, and new birth this makes us lovers too. We have to take the time, make the time, and establish the time that we will begin to love ourselves better and to love others better. Why not make a commitment to "do love" in little ways each day for a month? For what you do really does matter in the big picture of life. God has a grand design for each one of us, and there are people on this earth, in our sphere of influence, whom God is ready for us to love into the victorious realm of Christian living. Who have you loved recently?

A good place to begin is to ask yourself, how have you shown love to and for yourself? Have you done something nice, refreshing, or relaxing for yourself this month? What about that covenant you made with God to quit smoking, to quit cursing, to loose some weight, to begin to fast more, to stop gossiping or being so negative? Have you begun that "promised" exercise program yet? Have you sat down to read your Bible and begun the excellent habit of reading a good book? When was the last time you went to a movie or rented a comedy simply to laugh and enjoy yourself? Did you begin a time of prayer and meditation instead of hurrying to ask God's blessings just before you fall asleep each night? When we love ourselves, we begin to take some of these steps for self-improvement, and the Holy Spirit will help us, if we are willing.

The apostle Paul, writing in prison, knowing that his life was coming to an end, wanted to encourage his son in ministry, Timothy. He loved Timothy enough to tell him the truth. He recognized that Timothy was scared, watching his mentor serve time in prison and realizing that this might one day be his fate! Paul didn't jump on the young man but began to tell him how much he mattered to the people of faith. Paul also called on Timothy to remember his mother, Eunice, and to recall the life of his grandmother, Lois. Paul set pen to paper to help Timothy be reminded that the women before him had been influential with their lives of love and faith. And Paul said, "I am persuaded that this faith now lives in you" (2 Tim. 1:5).

What the apostle is saying here is that the time has come for Timothy to set his mind on what he wants to do with his life and who he wants to impact for the future. Paul says to him, "I know your people. And I know you too." We are kindred spirits with those who know us "into-me-see," intimately. When our passion is stirred, when we are determined to make a difference in the world, and when we are committed to being all that God has called us to be, the fire on the inside will be noticed by someone on the outside! For the only reason that we are called to be love and light in this world is to shine in all the places where light and love are absent.

Yes! Someone is watching YOU! Someone is waiting on you to influence them for the task ahead of them. God placed them in your life, put them in your personal space, and allowed them entry into your world so that you can make a permanent, positive impact upon them by your life. My assignment is to remind you that *it's your move!* Go ahead! Do something loving for both you and someone else. Try buying yourself a lovely bouquet of flowers, and get one for another person as well. No! You don't need any chocolates and, most likely, they don't either! But a prayer candle might be a nice idea, or what about a good book? It is your move to love! "Beloved, if your gift is serving, then serve; if it is teaching, then teach."

Beloved's Personal Journal

The apostle Paul writes to ensure that every gifted person recognizes just how important he or she is to the body of Christ. There are no big "I's" and little "you's" in the family of Jesus Christ. Each one of us has a spiritual gift or gifts, and the gift of love is shed abroad in each of our hearts! There is no way around it, out of it, or skipping it—we are called to be major examples of love to those with whom we have interactions, both in and out of the church.

Jesus was clear that he came to serve and not to be served. We seem to forget that serving is a primary function of our Christian duties. If all of us got that principle down pat, there would be more than enough love to go around. For the truth is that, as we give love away, it boomerangs back to us!

1. What function, activity, or event was going on when you first experienced the manifest love of God through your local church?

2. Have you ever been at a place, in your life when family love seemed to be very spare, missing, or absent? Define the time and your feelings.

3. How was love doled out in your childhood home?

4. When was the last time that you made a serious attempt to show love to a church member, co-worker, or good friend? What did you do for that person?

5. What major act of love has been shown to you in the past month?

8

HOLY HOKEY POKEY

Discover, develop and deploy
your spiritual gifts.

L. H.

Beloved, [if your gift] is to encourage,
then give encouragement; if it is giving, then give
generously; if it is to lead, do it diligently;
if it is to show mercy, do it cheerfully.

Romans 12:8 TNIV

ALL OF US CAN REMEMBER THE FUN DAYS OF PLAYING Hokey Pokey in kindergarten. Its purpose was to help make us aware of our body parts as well as teach us how to become winners. We were quick to grasp the reality that we were not a winner at the game of Hokey Pokey until we had put our whole self in! Many of us fail to realize that God is waiting on us to play holy Hokey Pokey too!

We may just want to put in our head, to offer our intellect—our opinions and our well-conceived and well-thought-out decisions. Just putting it in our head, however, is not good enough.

Many of us just want to put in our arms—our sweat equity—and have the many hours that we give to worthwhile volunteer efforts make us a winner. But that's not good enough.

Some of us want to put in our feet, with a willingness to go, to do, and to be the missionary at home and abroad—the mission project worker down the street or even the helping hand in foreign lands. But our feet simply won't make us a winner with God.

Holy Hokey Pokey requires all of us, including our *time*, our *talents*, and our *tithes*. Stewardship is not a matter of simply money. Stewardship is being a faithful disciple as an act of both our faith and our obedience to God's Word. We cannot pay others to do ministry for us. Regardless of the pastoral and support staff of our local congregation, each one of us has a ministry gift to execute. God's church is maintained by each of us being an active member of this volunteer army.

Stewardship includes the act of tithing, giving back to God at least 10 percent of what we have received. Certainly we cannot expect God to credit our faith account by the dollars that we give alone. But the One who made and maintains the world expects, anticipates, mandates, and commands that we work out our own salvation with our whole self involved in mission ministry during our lives. The apostle Paul began a serious reflection on the importance of our employing our spiritual gifts. He included the gift of giving among them. In order to win at being a Christian, our purse strings have to be saved and sanctified too!

In Mark 12: 41–43, we find Jesus sitting, watching, and longing for us to put our whole selves into the game of being church. Jesus really does want all of us—our arms and hands, our head, our feet and legs, our wallets, checkbooks, and purses! Isn't it odd that Jesus sat down to watch a woman moving with the offering line?

We know Jesus as a lover of people, a caller of people, a feeder of people, a healer of people, and even a talker with people. But one day Jesus became a people watcher to see who would win God's game of holy Hokey Pokey!

Jesus, who noticed their dress and demeanor as well as the motivations of their hearts, watched the wealthy and the proud. Jesus watched their posture as they paraded around the Temple to deposit their offerings in the treasury. There were no ushers. There were no polished brass offering plates. There were no large kettles or woven baskets to be passed around for a collection. For

God's instructions were, "Bring your God an offering!" To carry an offering was a personal symbol of thanksgiving and gratitude for all that had been received from the graciousness of a generous Creator. So the holy Hokey Pokey game was on and Jesus was sitting there, watching.

The folks came forth. Some threw in much to impress the Temple leadership. Some had their servants pour in large amounts so that the clanging sounds would indicate their generosity. Some had guards surrounding them to symbolize their stature in the community. And Jesus just sat and watched.

Whenever a rabbi sat, it was a sign of preparing to teach some lesson of great significance. Jesus wanted the disciples of all time to learn from his watching experience. As he watched in the midst of this hypocrisy, he saw a poor woman make her way toward the treasury.

This woman was not simply poor in that she was thought to be an insignificant and worthless female. This sister was poverty stricken. She had no male relatives to care for her. She was down to her very last. She was at the juncture of "what will I do next and how will I survive?" She had no food stamps. She had so subsidy program. She had no welfare reform on her side. All that she had left were two coins and a promise that God would provide! Could she win?

Common sense says that she should have kept the coins and tried to find several more. Common sense says she would have waited until after the Temple officials had received all the offerings and gone around quietly to see whether any loose coins had hit the floor during the collection. Common sense says give God one coin and save one for you. At least feed yourself a last, decent meal that could be purchased for one coin.

But, the scripture is clear. This poverty-stricken woman unwrapped her two coins and put them both in the offering. Jesus declared, "She just played God's holy Hokey Pokey. And she's a winner!" Our sister put her whole self in, even all that she had in her possession. And so Jesus said, "She gave more than all of the rest."

Jesus is yet sitting and watching and waiting. We have to contribute all that we have to offer. We have to unwrap our spiritual gifts and contribute what we have in ministry. We have to volunteer our time and not wait for "somebody else" to do the necessary ministry. And we have to at least begin to tithe, because God loves a cheerful giver.

Tithing is an equitable, fair, and responsible way of sharing what God has blessed us with. If we work full time, tithing is equitable. If we are on a fixed income, tithing is equitable. If we are on general assistance, tithing is equitable. If we receive an allowance, tithing is equitable. If we have a babysitting job or work at the local McDonald's, tithing is equitable. For 10 percent of what we receive remains the same from a dollar to a billion dollars!

Tithing is the answer to the psalmist's question, "What can I render unto God for all that I have received?" Tithing is the only instance where God says, "Let's make a deal. Bring the full tithe in . . . test me in this . . . see if I will not open the floodgates of heaven and pour out so much blessing that you will not have room for it" (Mal. 3:10 NIV). The woman that Jesus sat to watch took God's Word literally as her personal precious promise!

Jesus is yet watching to see what you and I will do. It's "whole self" time! "Beloved, if your gift is to encourage, then give encouragement; if it is giving, then give generously; if it is to lead, do it diligently; if it is to show mercy, do it cheerfully."

Beloved's Personal Journey

Paul's continuing emphasis on God's grace sets the agenda for our recognition that all we have comes from the generous hands of a gracious Sovereign. We are gifted, not by merit, but only by grace. When we refuse to utilize our spiritual gift, we show dishonor to the Creator! All that we have is on loan to us. We are merely stewards of God's belongings. We have absolutely *nothing* that we can claim. What God requires is that we tithe one tenth of our earnings back into the work of ministry, so that God might continue to supply our needs, bless us, and be gracious to us, over and over again!

1. When did you learn about the concept of giving God 10 percent?

2. Do you "tithe" from your gross income or your net income? Why?

3. Name a blessing experience that you *know* came about only due to "God's opening up the floodgates of heaven" on your behalf?

4. Explain to a new convert, a new member, or a coworker what tithing is all about.

9

BECOMING AUTHENTIC FOR CHRIST

There's nothing like the real thing!
God is love!
So let God be God in you!

L. H.

Beloved, let love be genuine;
abhor what is evil,
hold fast to what is good.

Romans 12:9 ESV

A YOUNG PREACHER WENT TO AN OLD PREACHER AND ASKED, "How can I get victory over pride and criticism?" The preacher said to him, "Go to the grave of Brother Jones, who recently passed away, and as you stand by the grave say all the nice things you can about him. Flatter him greatly."

Off to the graveyard the young preacher went to do as the old preacher had advised. Upon return the old preacher asked, "What did he say?" The answer: "Nothing. He's dead."

Then the old preacher said, "Go back out to the grave and criticize Brother Jones. Say every mean thing imaginable to him."

When the young preacher came back, the old preacher asked, "What did he say?" The young preacher said, "Nothing, He's dead!"

The old preacher said, "Reckoning ourselves dead with Christ, we will be unmoved by flattery or criticism."

Pray for me. I'm not there yet![1]

Don't laugh! For you have not arrived either! This is why all of us need the power of the gift of the Holy Spirit to be alive and operative in our lives! The older I grow, the more I am appreciative of the formation of the first church and our history in and with Jesus Christ, who was not moved by flattery or criticism either.

Paul reminds us that the church is about relationships! First, we know that we must have a relationship with God through Jesus Christ, and then, a relationship with the indwelling Holy Spirit. The church is about sharing! We are united around the globe through the blood of Jesus sacrificed to redeem all of us at Calvary. The church is about being the body of Christ, both gathered and scattered. God knows that we know how to do church together. We like to eat together. We like to sing together. We like to meet in the parking lot together. We like to call one another and run other folks down, together. Notice that I left "worship" out of our togetherness. For when we are truly in worship together, we experience the Love that is God. And we are then forced by the power of the Holy Spirit to pass that love along, after worship and during the week. Believers share one with another, in the Spirit, being the body of Christ.

It's so true that the call for flattery is worldwide. It's not relegated to one gender, race, ethnic group, or crowd. Our self-esteem needs to be enhanced; every now and then we all need a pat on the back. Yet flattery is most often used to pump up an individual who has not really done all that much out of the ordinary! Flattery is too often, in too many instances, old-fashioned butt kissing. For too many of us are yet "stuck" in "dat'll do" mode and don't push ourselves to excellence. Flattery will keep you working in that mode and not doing your best. Flattery is often a nice form of lying! Beware of those who come to you with flattery all the time. Know that they are seeking something from you. Be like Brother Jones and remain quiet.

The call to criticize is worldwide. It's not relegated to one gender, race, ethnic group, or crowd. Low self-esteem will cause many to run down, try to tear up, and make attempts to kill the influence of any "new" thing on the face of the earth! I know that all of us can use constructive criticism. I recognize that constructive criticism will allow my personal efforts to be improved by thoughts, ideas, and strategies that I have not even considered. But I'm not talking about constructive criticism. I'm addressing that old fashioned habit, every Sunday after church or daily after work, in the parking lot, discussing and pulling down some new and innovative idea. When folks come to us with destructive criticism, we need to be like Brother Jones and remain quiet.

In order to skip both the flattery, which is a lie, and the criticism that will be aimed at us as soon as our backs are turned, we need the power of the Holy Spirit at work in us, on us, through us, and in spite of us! "Spirit of the Living God, fall afresh on me. Spirit of the Living God, fall afresh on me. Melt me, mold me, fill me, use me. Spirit of the Living God, fall afresh on me."[2] This is a prayer. This is a plea. This is a petition. This is our energy that will allow us to go into places, deal with people, and see about issues without becoming a hindrance to the realm of God.

Paul is clear as he instructs the church at Rome, "Let love be genuine; hate what is evil, hold fast to what is good."

"When the apostles in Jerusalem heard that Samaria had accepted the word of God, they sent Peter and John to them" (Acts 8:14 NIV). Now, we know that the Jews and the Samaritans were related by blood. But since the Samaritans were those who had married the Assyrians, enemies of the Jews, the Jews were hateful, unforgiving, and not in relationship at all! We can be assured that it was only the power of the Holy Spirit, who was able to touch hearts, minds, and spirits, that the disciples sent two of their top leaders into "enemy" territory. Thank God for Jesus Christ, who sent back the gift of the Holy Spirit to break down the walls between all of our different factions of the body of Christ!

The disciples went to share what they had with those folks who had been their relatives and their "enemies" for long generations. The disciples went to help unify the body of Christ. For the love of God breaks down barriers of all sorts; it erases hostility and unites us in Jesus Christ. We all have the same, efficacious blood covering us. We all have the same name, Christian, connecting us. And, we all have the same Holy Spirit available to us as a gift!

It's been the keeping power of the Holy Spirit that had me raised as a Pentecostal, educated and ordained as a United Methodist, and able to worship freely in a Baptist congregation! God is all in all and through all who lift up the name of Jesus!

The early church gives us our first portrait of how to eat, live, learn, and grow spiritually into community. Church history provides us with a wealth of experiences to show how nations, countries, and denominations have grown and spread because of the sharing nature of God's people. Our own country is a prime example.

Do you know the history of your denomination and local congregation? When was the last time that your local congregation held a day or activity to uplift your history makers? So much has been done by so many generous souls, and we say way too little about it! Many folks have sacrificed, given, and left legacies so that you and I might inhabit the buildings and the grounds we "claim" as our own. It was the power and fire and energizing power of the Holy Spirit that enabled folks with so little to achieve so much! Thanks be unto God that the same Holy Spirit has not grown tired of giving us the will and the abilities to share what we have with each other! The beat of God's church moves on as we continue to let love be genuine! "Beloved, let love be genuine; abhor what is evil, hold fast to what is good."

Beloved's Personal Journey

The old Coca-Cola commercial used to say, "Ain't nothing like the real thing, baby. Ain't nothing like the real thing!" I wonder if the jingle writers had read Romans 12. This is surely the apostle Paul's strict, firm, and steadfast command to the church at Rome: don't fake God's love! Seems as if Paul didn't adhere to the AA slogan of "Fake it 'til you make it!"

The struggle between good and evil, between God and Satan, didn't just begin. The war was declared when Satan decided to challenge God and got thrown out of heaven with one third of the heavenly host following. This war rages on, and now we are duty bound to express, manifest, and evidence God's love from within us to the whole world. When our mind is transformed, renewed, and changed by the power of the Holy Spirit, love is instilled within us to be distilled into the world.

1. When did you fully realize that you "loved" someone who had not mattered to you before?

2. How do you recognize genuine (not pretending, not play-acting) love?

3. Describe "the love of God for you" to someone who feels unlovable.

4. When was the last time that God's love was made visible through you?

10

STRETCHING OUR LOVE

*Show God and the world exactly
what you're working with. It's all about love!*

L. H.

*Beloved, love one another with [mutual] affection;
outdo one another in showing honor.*

Romans 12:10 ESV

ARE YOU FAMILIAR WITH THE NONPROFIT ORGANIZATION Balm in Gilead? Its mission is "to improve the health status of the African Diaspora by building the capacity of faith communities to address life threatening diseases, especially HIV/AIDS." Pernessa Seals, an impressive, short, but strong African American woman, who worked for the Center for Disease Control before founding Balm in Gilead, saw up close and personal what HIV/AIDS was doing to the black communities while the black church remained silent! Little Sista took it upon herself to start a movement that is now twenty years old.

On the first Sunday in December, the Balm in Gilead encourages black churches to recognize all of their members, living and dead, who have been afflicted by this horrible disease. It makes no difference how people contract HIV/AIDS! Whether it's from homosexual relationships, needle exchanges in drug use, unmonitored blood transfusions, or brothers on the down low, it's a killer that is affecting all of us. There are people in our pews

(YES! Yours too!), preachers in pulpits, musicians on benches, singers in choirs, ushers on the floor, and officers in our local congregations (YES! Yours too!) who are suffering with a killer disease and afraid to come out of the closet for prayer, support, and comfort. It's time for every one of our local congregations to do something significant about the silence regarding HIV/AIDS.

Prophetess Mallie Nichols of St. Louis, Missouri, forwarded me the following e-mail that speaks truth. Please read it slowly. It could be from a member of anyone of our congregations.

> To those of you who are single or married, saved or not saved, this is for you. I am a thirty-five-year old brother dying of HIV/AIDS. I would like to share my testimony with you. I am an owner of a mortgage company in Atlanta, Georgia. I own a 1999 Jaguar and I also own a $350,000 beautiful home in Cobb County. I have a beautiful lady who is deeply in love with me, and a loving family. But most importantly, I have Jesus.
>
> This note is just a wake-up call to all single brothers and sisters who are professing to be Christians but don't want to be complete in Jesus. Brothers, I had a beautiful young lady who loves the Lord and worships the ground I walk on. But I still wasn't quite happy because sometimes I would see another sister with a Coca-Cola bottle shape, and I just wanted to hit it. Because I was using a condom I thought that I wouldn't catch the killer AIDS! But, guess what? I did. And the person I caught it from was a girl that I knew well. But the condom came off, and now I am dying of AIDS!
>
> Yes, I wore a condom. But, yes, it did happen. God gives us time after time to straighten our lives up. I do know the Lord in the pardon of my sins. I've been saved now for seven years. I found out seven months ago that I had the [HIV] virus, and now I have full-blown AIDS. And I want you all to know that I have never been with another man. I really didn't think that I was doing any-

thing wrong, because I would tell the women who I would deal with about the woman I love. I thought that was good enough. But it wasn't. I am a good man and also a God-fearing man but my weakness was women.

I really wasn't out there like you may think I was. But every once and a while I would see something I wanted to try. My girlfriend is a praying woman. I know now that she was intimate with me because she loved me and she wanted to make me happy.

Now I've given AIDS to the woman I love (who has been faithful to me) because of lust. Brothers and sisters, what I am telling you is that God is tired of us hurting each other and using each other for self gratification. God has given me my home, my dream car, and a beautiful woman, and I took it all for granted. I've been tithing for seven years. I am the chairman of my Deacon Board. But when I told my pastor I had AIDS, he could not believe it because of the way I would carry myself.

Brothers . . . if you have a sister who loves the Lord and who loves you for who you are and not for what you look like and not for what you have, cherish her. Sisters . . . if you have a brother who loves the Lord, love him and cherish him. My life has been altered.

I've been with my lady since I was twenty, and I've always used my young age as an excuse for not being loyal and not settling down with the woman I loved. I was being a hypocrite thinking that I was missing something, and not realizing that I had a good woman who loved and adored me.

I wish I had been a real man and had appreciated the good woman God had sent me by not making excuses and dedicating my life to her. I would love to travel and marry this beautiful young lady—but now I can't. I've embarrassed my family, my church, and my friends. But I was hardheaded and now I must suffer. God is cleaning up. Stop playing with God. God is revealing the secrets of us Christians. Brothers and sisters, we don't have to have so many "friends," you know what we call them. "The ones we are planning to sleep with but haven't yet."

We often say that we don't want anyone to know our business, but God is about to reveal some things, especially among us young people. We think so carnally. But we say that we have been transformed. We have been transformed from what we want to be transformed from. Let's be real. God knows that the opposite sex attracts us. And he knows the desires we have for each other, but we don't have to have multiple partners. If I could do it all over again, I would marry the woman I love and live happy forever. But now I can't! But you can!

Singles, I gotta tell you, it's not worth it. I love you all! Get rid of casual sex. And pray for the strength to be celibate. This testimony is really deep. After you've read this, think about yourself. Could this have been you? Some of you may not relate, but think about anything that you are doing right now that is not of God. You may not have anything to do with premarital sex or a sexual affair, but sin is sin and everything done in the dark shall come to light. We are living in the last and final days, and pretending to be saved is not going to cut it.

Professing that Jesus Christ is Lord and yet worshiping the devil every chance you get will lead you to the same path as me. Sex for those who are saved must be with your OWN wife or husband. That includes necking and petting, touching, oral sex, phone or Internet sex, and even fantasizing. Get your mind out of the gutter and put it in the Word of God and you'll have great success. Don't, and you'll have great woe.

I love God and am so thankful for all that has been done in my life. Therefore, I'm passing this message on. Yes, I do love Jesus, who has forgiven me of the repeated sins. That forgiveness does not cancel out the consequences, at least not so far. But that's on me. Still, God, source of my existence, and Jesus Christ, my Savior, keep me functioning each day and are letting me share my story with you. I'm telling it like it REALLY is to help somebody. Without God, I would be nothing. Without God, I am nothing. But with God, I can do all things through Christ Jesus who gives me strength (Phil. 4:13). Friends, be positive, be progressive and take the time to make a positive difference in someone's life today!

When an educated Jewish man asked Jesus what he must do to inherit eternal life, Jesus directed him to say what was written in the Law. "He answered, 'Love the Lord your God with all your heart and with all your soul and with all your strength and with all your mind'; and, 'Love your neighbor as yourself'" (Luke 10:27). When the man asked Jesus who his neighbor was, Jesus told the story of the good Samaritan. He essentially told the educated Jewish man and us to stretch our love!

Jesus said that we cannot limit our love, our resources, our community, or our prayerful support to just those who fit our "criteria." I close with another tale of wisdom from the e-mail circuit: There was a farmer who grew award-winning corn. Each year he entered his corn in the state fair where it won a blue ribbon.

One year a newspaper reporter interviewed him and learned something interesting about how he grew it. The reporter discovered that the farmer shared his prize-winning seed corn with his neighbors.

"How can you afford to share your best seed corn with your neighbors when they are entering corn in competition with yours each year?" the reporter asked.

"Why sir," said the farmer, "didn't you know that the wind picks up pollen from the ripening corn and swirls it from field to field? If my neighbors grow inferior corn, cross-pollination will steadily degrade the quality of my corn. If I am to grow good corn, I must help my neighbors grow good corn."

This farmer is very much aware of the connectedness of life. His corn cannot improve unless his neighbor's corn also improves. So it is in other dimensions of our lives. Those who choose to be at peace must help their neighbors to be at peace. Those who choose to live well must help others to live well, for the value of a life is measured by the lives it touches. And those who choose to be happy must help others to find happiness, for the welfare of each is bound up with the welfare of all. The lesson for each of us is this: if we are to grow good corn, we must help our neighbors grow good corn too![1]

Let's think of ways that we can stretch ourselves, our church groups, our social groups, our community groups so that every time the first Sunday in December comes, we have some solid plans for how our congregations, organizations, social groups, and civic groups can do something that is positive, progressive, and makes a permanent, positive difference in someone's life who is affected by HIV/AIDS! "Beloved, love one another with mutual affection; outdo one another in showing honor." Show God and the world exactly what you're working with! It really is all about love!

Beloved's Personal Journal

Evil is a constant threat to the people of God. Yet God so loved the world that Jesus was given so that believers might have help, assistance, power, and deliverance to just say "No" to sin. The apostle Paul was well aware that in even the most close-knit families there is always a jockeying for position, power, and favor. So he wants all Christians to utilize their privilege and responsibility to love others with reckless abandon, so he states that they are to "outdo" each other in love. In this manner, it will be difficult for evil to win!

1. What is your take on the Christian church and HIV/AIDS?

2. Do you know a brother or a sister who needs to read the letter printed in this chapter that the AIDS victim has written? How will you approach that person? Describe your action plan.

3. When was the last time that you were forced, by the Holy Spirit, to overlook an unloving or unkind deed aimed at you? How loving was your response?

4. When was the last time that someone was forced, by the Holy Spirit, to overlook an unloving or unkind deed that you did? How loving was that person's response?

11

SPIRITUAL DISCIPLINES

It's all about how you serve.

L. H.

Beloved, do not lag in zeal, be ardent in spirit; serve God.

Romans 12:11

My beloved spouse, Mista Chuck, is a private pilot. I have fond memories of our first flight in a little Piper Cub. I asked about our connection with the airport. I didn't hear the radio speaking from ground control and I wanted to make sure that we didn't accidentally hit another plane, or get hit by one either! It was then that Mista Chuck told me that we are on a "see and be seen mission!" This meant that he was watching out for other planes at our level and he was "hoping/wishing/believing" that other pilots would be on the alert for him! Not only was this a scary way for me to fly, it's altogether contrary to the way that Jesus expects us to live!

Jesus, our role model, is so helpful as we reflect upon his teachings and check out our personal lives. It's so easy for me to compare myself with others around me, for I can always find some method or some action that I can do "better" or at least "not as bad" as them! As Christians, however, we are not to be on a "see and be seen mission!" We *are* to be seen as lights in the world. When it comes to a vital relationship with Christ, however, we are to do what we do, almost in the dark! Honestly, in this particular venture of "doing good," it's alright to be invisible!

"Be careful not to do your acts of righteousness before others, to be seen by them. If you do, you will have no reward from God. So when you give to the needy, do not announce it, . . . as the hypocrites do, to be honored by others. I tell you the truth, they have received their reward in full. But, when you give to the needy, do not let your left hand know what your right hand is doing, so that your giving may be in secret. Then God, who sees what is done in secret, will reward you. And, when you pray, do not be like the hypocrites. . . . But, when you pray, go into your room, close the door, and pray" (Matt. 6:1–6a).

Our tension here is to do all the good that we can, for all the people that we can, wherever we can and to be exquisitely quiet about it! Jesus teaches us that when we receive the big pats on the back, that's it. When we get the cut glass awards, loud accolades, "atta girl" and "good boy," high-five strokes, we have gotten all that we are going to get!

And if you're like me, I want my "thank you cards"! I want my record of giving. I enjoy being stroked for going out of my way, for doing the over-and-above job! It's the human nature and ego in me! I like being noticed. I want to be seen. And God knows that I'm looking to see what you're doing! But, this is not the spiritual way that Jesus teaches me and it requires my daily, constant openness to the Holy Spirit working in me, on me, and through me to help me do it the right way. This is where it becomes mandatory that I practice the spiritual disciplines of prayer, meditation on God's Word, fasting, and singing hymns, anthems, and spiritual songs to keep me on the Jesus track and not the "see and be seen" tour!

> It takes courage to refrain from gossip when others about you delight in it; to stand up for an absent person who is being abused; to live honestly within your means and not dishonestly on the means of others; to be a real

man, a true woman, by holding fast to your Christian ideals when it causes you to be looked upon as strange and peculiar. It takes courage to be talked about and yet remain silent when a word would justify you in the view of others, but which you cannot speak without injury to another. It takes courage to refuse to do a thing which is wrong, though others do it; to dress according to your income and to deny yourself what you cannot afford to buy; and to live always according to your convictions.[1]

What this anonymous author calls "courage," I tend to call the Holy Spirit. We cannot make it without the power of the Holy Spirit working in us, on us, through us, and even in spite of us! For the Holy Spirit is God present in us! The Holy Spirit comes to bring to our mind the teachings of Jesus and to help us "want" to do the right things! And the Holy Spirit gives us the ability to do what Jesus has taught us, what he role modeled by his life, death, and resurrection!

I pray that the words from a little song will stay in our spirit. I pray that when we begin to want applause, notice, and recognition this short prayer hymn will break in upon us: "Breathe on me, Breath of God. Fill me with life anew, that I may love what thou does love, and do what thou would do!"[2] May our practice of the spiritual disciplines, including singing this prayer song, draw us closer to Jesus Christ. As we move closer to Christ, less of us and more of him will be seen. Beloved, practice being a secret saint this week! "Do not lag in zeal, be ardent in spirit, serve God." It really is all about how you promise to serve others, and then it's all about how you follow through!

Beloved's Personal Journal

The body of Christ is to be the "power and light" company in the world! The Holy Spirit provides the power and we are known as the lights of this world! There is no way that we can be Christian and kissing cousins with evil! We cannot tolerate evil. We must hate evil, for it is at war with God! Paul expects, anticipates, and encourages every believer to present an all-out attack on anything that smells, looks, or behaves like evil.

In every family, in every congregation, and in every fellowship we know that evil will rear its head and act out! The family of God, however, is admonished to banish evil with good. Genuine love and demonstrated Christ-like behaviors will cause evil to flee!

1. The only reason for a light bulb is to chase away the darkness. When was the last time that you were forced to "be" the light in a situation?

2. In the games of tennis and golf, it is essential that the players follows through on their stroke. How do you follow through when you are called upon to serve a family member, neighbor, or friend?

3. Reflect upon the last time that your Christian journey demanded "courage" of you.

12

B E L O V E D ?

Be steadfast in prayer.
Use words only as a last resort!

L. H.

Beloved, rejoice in hope,
be patient in suffering, persevere in prayer.

Romans 12:12

WHEN I HEAR THE WORD "BELOVED," I IMMEDIATELY THINK OF the book by Toni Morrison, made into a movie by Oprah Winfrey. I tried reading the book. I never saw the movie. I did buy a book about Oprah's making of the movie, but haven't read it either. Toni Morrison writes in a strange, twisting, and mysterious manner and most of the time, as with Alice Walker, I cannot keep up with her train of thought! But I was shocked, as was Oprah, when her movie bombed. She's a woman who knows how to make money. But the movie *Beloved* was a flop at the theater. Now, she says that she learned much from making it and that she's no longer upset about it not being a hit. Maybe one day, when I'm completely bored, with absolutely nothing else to do, I might rent the video and see what it's all about! Yet, like the apostle Paul, I like the word "Beloved."

It refers to a person who is in the state of being loved. A "beloved" individual has been set apart as significant, special, and outstanding. The beloved one is worthy of loving and has some qualities that are lovable. A "beloved" person is one who is highly thought of, esteemed, regarded with tenderness and often with great affection. One who is "beloved" receives much attention and many accolades and most likely has multiple accomplishments under his or her belt. When I think of a "beloved" person in our local community, the name Mother Ella Mary Sims comes immediately to mind.

One of our local educational institutions, Aquinas College, elected to vote Mrs. Sims as a trustee emeritus. The date of the event was heralded with white and gold invitations, signifying that a scholarship was going to be established in her name, and therefore the price of the evening began at $150. With the exception of receiving "free" tickets to the opening of the new, downtown Convention Center, Mista Chuck and I don't attend many events of this nature. We do like to eat at home and $150 will feed us, Giraurd, and Duchess for at least a week or two!

Yet, due to Mother Sims being so "beloved" by me, so respected by me, and so highly thought of by me, we sacrificed and bought one ticket to the event. Mista Chuck could not attend, for I didn't want to have to be forced to visit friends and family for the rest of the month when dinner time approached! The reception was standing room only, and, there were few empty seats at the dinner. This is what happens when you are "beloved" by the community!

Mother Sims' children had gathered from across the country. Out of seven sons, five are ministers, one of whom gave the invocation, another raised a toast and named his mom Reverend Sims. A grandson gave remarks (preached) about her regal, royal character, while her daughter, Dr. Mary Alice Sims of California, prayed the benediction. The Honorable Judge Benjamin Logan and Ms. Mary Alice Williams, CEO of Arbor Circle, both gave testimonies about this "beloved" legend, who raised all of her children along with others' children, had remained at one local congregation, investing in lives, helping neighbors, training politicians, promoting others, and finally earning her college degree after age fifty!

Ella Sims has had her tests, trials, and tribulations. Life has not always been kind or fair to her. Her spouse was not always wonderful. Yet, she stayed, prayed, and persevered. Her children did their share of antics, got into trouble, and broke her heart. Yet, she stayed, prayed, and persevered. Death came to visit too often; money was short too often; pain was a companion, too often; and troubles kept knocking on her door. Yet, through it all, she stayed focused. She practiced the art of prayer, intercession, and spiritual warfare. She persevered and encouraged others to do the very same thing in the face of overwhelming odds. She never gave up. She never said, "I quit!" She kept on pushing and sometimes she shoved her way through!

The evening to honor her was outstanding. When Mother Sims came to the podium, there was a standing ovation! In her soft-spoken, gracious manner, she thanked the audience for loving her. It was a night to behold as a beloved woman was praised for her life-giving nature to all she encounters. She has experienced some heavy blows like the rest of us. But nothing seems to dampen her spirits, delay her smile, or keep her off the phone, encouraging and praying with and for others. She has proven herself steadfast and dependable over the years. The community gathered to say, "Thanks!"

It was in community that Jesus was called "Beloved" by God. For the community must witness your life, testify to your loving deeds, and be the recipients of your gracious acts. As Jesus, who knew no sin, was allowing his crazy cousin, John the Baptizer, to bring him up out of the Jordan River, a dove flew down to represent the Holy Spirit, and a loud, booming voice was heard by all who were present. "You are my son, the Beloved. With you I am well pleased" (Mark 1:11).

Although John had called all of the townspeople who were running out to the water to "see" the new thing called water baptism, and John had the audacity to call them a bunch of snakes, he gave his stamp of approval to Jesus by baptizing him and stating that he felt unworthy to tie his shoes. And that big, booming, thunderous voice from heaven also gave Jesus approval by naming him "Beloved"! Jesus was one who was constantly in a state of being loved by God. And now this charge of being called "Beloved" is at each of our doors.

Mother Ella Mary Sims has lived to witness her own funeral eulogy! Her life was held up for review and honored. There is very little left to say about this eighty-one-year-old saint of God. Her children have spoken. Her family has spoken. The college has spoken. The community has spoken. She is beloved! The question now comes: What about you and me? Are we beloved? This question asks whether we are in a consistent state of receiving gifts of love back at us from all the love that we have given out? For love given is always love returned!

We are social creatures, always touching people, interacting with both the known and the unknown in our communities. Try "being love" this week! Remember, it's little acts that count too, smiling, speaking, and doing nice things for those around us. Are you beloved? "Beloved, rejoice in hope, be patient in suffering, preserve in prayer." The community is watching how you live. Your day to be named Beloved will come. Just keep walking the talk of being like Christ.

Beloved's Personal Journal

There are tangible, visible attributes that can be characterized by those whom we call and name beloved. It is not that they do not experience difficulties in their lives; it is that they know to continue steadfast in prayer and to follow the lead of the Holy Spirit. Prayer is our privilege to be in communication with God. We are invited to "come boldly before the throne of grace" to receive all that we need to remain beloved to God and to those whom we serve.

1. Describe the most beloved person you know.

2. What characteristics of a beloved individual do you evidence?

3. When do you spend quality time in prayer?

4. What methods of prayer do you utilize?

5. Who taught you to pray?

13

MEETING HUMAN NEEDS?

Extending our love is essential.

L. H.

Beloved, contribute to the needs of the saints;
extend hospitality to strangers.

Romans 12:13

AS AN AFRICAN AMERICAN WOMAN, I HAVE BEEN TAUGHT HOW
to help other people. As an African American Christian woman,
I have been shown how to do the ministry of outreach. As an
African American Christian woman who is also United
Methodist, worshiping Baptist, and reared Church of God in
Christ (Pentecostal to the max!), I have seen that the local church
talks a good game of meeting human needs. But talk is so cheap!
The world is watching for Christians to walk the talk of our
being Christ-like. How are you measuring up?

Only one time in all of Holy Scriptures does Jesus talk about
eschatology or the end of time. Only one time, with all of his
marvelous teaching, does Jesus open up to the disciples about exactly what God will be looking for on judgment day. Only one
time, with all of the parables, the miracles, the conversations, and
the involvement with people does Jesus stop and set forth how
the measures for our meeting human needs will affect our ever-
after. It's recorded in Matthew 25, where Jesus describes the

sheep and the goats. Let me hurry to tell you what category we want to be in at the judgment! We want to be counted as sheep!

The United Methodist Church is filled with program after program. My denomination knows how to fill up millions of sheets of paper calling us to be actively involved in social concern: feeding the hungry; clothing the naked; crying out for justice; being ecumenical and open to other religious bodies; marching in protests and speaking out on political issues. United Methodists are divided over whether homosexuality is sin. United Methodists are divided over whether or not abortion, drinking to excess, or racism is sin. But United Methodists do believe in the social gospel, sometimes to the exclusion of Jesus Christ!

On the other hand, there are the pious congregations I've watched over the years who are concerned for themselves alone. "Us 'four' and no more!" At one of the congregations I served in Illinois, the chair of trustees bragged about how they put the polling place out of "their" church! I have been privileged to travel the country, doing research on congregations in every region, and I have sadly discovered that we tend to forget that Matthew 25 is in the book.

We have a serious tension between religious piety and our intentional involvement with social concerns such as poverty, hunger, justice, and compassion for the downtrodden and oppressed. Yet with the name Christian, we are called to express our devotion and commitment to Christ and to be in relationship with all of those we meet and who need us in our world. Paul refers us back to the sayings of Jesus in the book of Matthew. Paul dares us to open our eyes, to see the needy, and to respond in love! Paul sort of draws us a line:

Life ___ Eternity _____

With practical application as his intent, Paul says that what we do with sharing in this life will determine where we spend eternity! Jesus explained it like this: "[God] will reply, 'I tell you the truth, whatever you did for one of the least of these, my sisters and my brothers, you did for me" (Matt. 25:40 NIV). These are the sheep. These are the ones who will end up on the right hand of God! They will be stunned. They will be shocked. They will be speechless. For they understood that they were simply doing good to someone less fortunate! Their hearts of loving compassion made them go out of their way and offer help to a sibling, regardless of race, color, economic status, political party, or gender.

This does not mean that the sheep tried to take care of all the world's problems. This does not mean that the sheep didn't care for themselves, for their families, and for their local congregations. But it means that care, on behalf of Jesus Christ, extended beyond their door and their local gathering place in the name of God!

I'm learning, as an African American black Christian woman who chose to become United Methodist, that God does not expect me to give away all that I need. This is a pious, but foolish act! I have to love me enough to take care of me and mine first. But, in order for me to have something to give, I must be willing to live with less for me and for mine! It's been a bitter pill to swallow, for I never thought that I would ever get "too much!"

Well, this leaves us with the goats! The goats are those who have closed up their eyes and cannot see any need but their own! The goats are those who say, "I made it and so can anyone who wants to do so." The goats are those who have closed their ears to the pleas for justice, the hunger that rumbles in too many stomachs, and the prayer petitions that people within their own congregation make every Sunday. Jesus says that the goats will be separated, eternally, from God! "[God] will reply, 'I tell you the truth, whatever you did not do for one of the least of these, you did not do for me. Then, they [the goats] will go away to eternal punishment, but the righteous [the sheep] to eternal life" (Matt. 45–46 NIV). What a bitter pill this is to swallow!!!

Let's not be local congregations who can "see and hear" but will not act on behalf of those in need, both in and outside of their doors. If people come to us with specific needs, let's not be the "goats" and just call a committee to discuss those needs, with no action taken! So, little sheep, I suggest that you be on the lookout for Jesus among the poor, the downtrodden, and the marginalized. And, little sheep, I also suggest that you be on the lookout for Jesus in the wealthy supervisor, the person who cuts you off in traffic, and that little nasty neighborhood brat who keeps running across your lawn! For the day of judgment will soon come. God will then divide the sheep from the goat. No excuses allowed!

Be on the lookout for where Jesus is hiding in your very midst! Don't miss him! Extending our love is essential! "Beloved, contribute to the needs of the saints; extend hospitality to strangers."

Beloved's Personal Journal

The apostle Paul had this thing about giving, sharing, and distributing to the needy among church members. He seems to follow in the steps of Jesus Christ, who talked much about money, missions, and giving. Since we now better understand that all that we have is on loan to us from God, it should be much easier to open our hearts and our wallets, longing, yearning, and willing to divide our resources. Paul saw all possessions as gracious gifts that were to be used for the glory and honor of God and the benefit of the people of God. The essence of evil is to have and to withhold!

1. Name the time that someone, not in your family, came to your "aid."

2. Name the last time that you became a benefactor to someone outside of your family.

3. To be hospitable means literally to "pursue the stranger with love"! Reflect upon your most recent act of hospitality.

4. Describe your capacity to care for members of the body of Christ.

14

WE ARE THE HEALERS

This strategy goes against all that is within us!
However, we can win!

L. H.

Bless those who persecute you:
bless and do not curse.

Romans 12:14 NIV

WE ARE MEMBERS OF A CULTURE THAT CAN BE MEAN AND CRUEL, a society that continues to practice treating each other too harshly. Too often we treat each other as if we were each other's enemy, when the truth is that we are family by divine design. We will turn on our spouses, our children, our coworkers, and our neighbors, as if they are people against whom we have to protect ourselves. But God would have us communicate and be in relationship with one another; that's what counts toward eternity.

Our attacking one another is not productive! When we are negative in our thinking, our speech, and our conversations, we create an energy field that tends to cause us more problems, not fewer. As Christian adults we have to learn better ways to love one another! It's time out for fighting or avoiding issues. It's time out for cussing folks out and giving away pieces of our minds! We don't have enough to spare any longer! It takes all that we can do to make it one day at a time.

It's time out for "withholding" love. It's time to give love away, freely. We should have discovered by now that we cannot "control" anyone else's behavior. Each one of us was sent to this earth to learn our own spiritual life lessons. Everyone else has a personal agenda set by God, too. It's time for each one of us to be transformed by the power of God's amazing love, God's unconditional acceptance, God's approval, God's personal, divine acknowledgment of our lives and our destinies, as well as God's validation of our lives by the breath, energy, and spirit that is alive within us today.

It's time for each one of us to teach others how to both heal and transform any and all situations through the power of love. Once again, events in the aftermath of natural disasters such as hurricanes Katrina and Rita have shown the world that things will escalate out of control when neglect, disrespect, and negative judgment have been the feedback a group of people have received their entire life. The results of years of extensive neglect, judgment, minimalization, and being virtually invisible create an "inhumanity" that the world has now viewed with television coverage. Yet you and I, Jesus ambassadors, have been chosen to help create a world of peace.

We cannot be peacemakers if we judge each other and ourselves harshly. Therefore, we must practice giving love away, especially when we are most irritated or in fear. And we must practice forgiving others in order to have a ripple affect of peace in our lives.

How do you forgive the unforgivable? How do you stop fighting people who do stupid, nasty, cruel, mean-spirited things? How do you deal with people who abuse and control? How do you stop running away from and avoiding conversations with people you fear will harm you? How do we live worthy lives? I'm so glad that you asked me.

Seek first to find God. God is everywhere! God is not confined to our churches, our synagogues, and our temples on Saturday or Sunday morning. God is omnipresent, everywhere at the same time, wanting to be acknowledged as Sovereign, wanting to be affirmed as Creator, wanting to be listened to, talked to, and followed willingly. Today, actually look at your family members, coworkers, and neighbors, for God is there as well. The *imago dei*, the very image of God, is in every individual born into the world. God is only one breath away at any time!

Second, we must seek to learn how to love ourselves better! All of us need some "me" time and some "we" time. All of us need to reach out and to touch others in love. The reasons that many of us fail to reach out is that we have bought into an inferiority complex. But the devil is a lie! It was Africans who were created in the Garden of Eden. It was Africans who created the pyramids. It was Africans who created math, medicine, and pharmacies. We need to learn how to truly be black and proud because God loves those whom God created in black flesh!

We show our love when we have black art in our homes, read the black heritage Bible, and study our culture and pass it along. We show love for ourselves when we teach our grandchildren about their legacy and make them sit with us to watch documentaries, weekly movies that uplift and uphold the struggle for civil rights. We show our love for our heritage when we buy from our own entrepreneurs, vote to ensure good leaders, walk our neighborhoods and talk to our neighbors to keep crime, drugs, and the lowlifes out! We show our love for ourselves when we sing, play, and keep alive the legacy of good black music, the hymns, the anthems, and the good old Motown sounds!

And, finally, we must seek to understand, and then to be understood as a loving person, the results of a right relationship with God through Jesus Christ and the indwelling of the amazing Holy Spirit. When we have a personal relationship with Jesus Christ, it is a relationship that is based on God forgiving us for the sin of rebellion in our original parents in the Garden of Eden. Without forgiveness, there would be no salvation! Jesus came in order that God might forgive us! When we accept Jesus Christ into our hearts, we too must put into practice that art of letting go and forgiving whatever it was that others have done to us. When we forgive, we are not condoning what happened to us, we are simply giving what happened away into the capable hands of a loving God.

Way back in the early 1700s, Ms. Hannah More began to work on the issue of abolishing slavery. She wrote many books and tracts and lectured about the evil that the slave trade fostered, as well as it being a sinful practice, especially among the people of God. In one of her tracts she wrote: "Forgiveness is the economy of the heart . . . forgiveness saves the expense of anger, the cost of hatred, the waste of spirits."[1] Both our spirit and the spirits of those we hold in unforgiveness can be freed to become more than we have ever anticipated when we release old anger, hurt, and grudges. When we learn how to let go of the need for revenge, the desire to "pay back," and the tendency to hold our pain close and intensely, God will work in us and on us to move through the process of forgiving and moving ahead with our life.

God really does have our backs. God has promised to take care of all those who have hurt us, "dissed" us, made our lives miserable, and caused us to feel bad about the divine design that God created us to become! This is the matter of walking by faith into a new future and living worthy of all that we have received!

Why don't we adopt a neighbor, a church member, a retired coworker, or a former classmate and covenant to keep in touch? In seventh grade I walked to school and walked home with Barbara Jean Baker Vinson VanBuren. Today, almost fifty years later, we continue to walk together. She's my closest friend. She's my bosom buddy. We call one another. We send cards to one another. We had our kids together. We married and divorced together. We are united and together we stand! Barbara Jean is paralyzed today and sits in a wheel chair, often confined and bound to her home. I'm thankful for another of our high school classmates, Rev. Morris Cruse, who keeps up with her. I'm grateful for our third partner, Elizabeth Clark Brown, who will call to see about her. Barbara Jean is a worthy candidate of adoption for phone calls and visits. People like Barbara Jean are all around us. Each of us can adopt a peer!

A worthy life is one where you are giving yourself away by investing in others. Are you volunteering and helping a youth, a more senior citizen, or a little child? So many people have given so very much for us to be where we are today. We have no choice but to give back in worthy ways.

A worthy life is one where you learn to exercise more and to take care of your physical temple. A worthy life is one where you take your meds as prescribed, pay your life and health insurance, and stop worrying other folks with your stubborn ways. A worthy life is where we learn how to tithe our income and to trust God to make our way smooth. Beloved, we cannot depend upon Social Security; pensions or 401Ks. But, we can depend upon the faithfulness of God!

A worthy life is where we go to worship more than on Christmas, Mother's Day, and Easter. A worthy life is where we give our whole self over to the love of God; where we repent of our sin; where we confess Jesus as Sovereign and Savior; where we ask the Holy Spirit to come in and abide, lead, guide, and control us day by day.

A worthy life is when we can recognize, realize, and appreciate that it was God who gave us to each other. We have been through the storms and the rains; but God has kept us. We have endured heartaches and pains, but God has kept us. We have seen the world change and yet remain the same. Today we can testify that nothing has separated us from the love of God in Christ Jesus. The stresses and strains of life have not and will not divide or conquer that worthy "we can do it" spirit that resides deep down on the inside. I pray that it will always be the same as we learn to put Paul's words into practice: "Bless those who persecute you; bless and do not curse them!"

Beloved's Personal Journal

Isn't it easy to smile at a cute little baby? Isn't it wonderful to watch the antics of a charming two- or three-year-old child? How delightful is it to enjoy a group of happy, playing, giggling little girls or rough-housing little boys? The issue is that they grow up and become aggravating, even ugly-acting adults!

It is not easy to "bless" those who do evil toward us. It is not our first nature to offer kind, tender, loving words and acts of kindness toward them! But the apostle Paul was persuaded that with the transforming, changing, and renewing of our hearts, from the inside outward, we could come to the place where we could act like Jesus and walk in his footsteps who prayed for those who did him the greatest evil of all.

1. How is this particular passage being worked out in your personal life?

2. When was the last time the evil of selfishness raised its ugly head in you?

3. In what area of your life do you need to work on becoming more "worthy"?

4. Without forgiveness there would be no Christian religion! Who needs your forgiveness today and why?

15

SWIFT TRANSITIONS

*We can celebrate even while in our down times
and spaces. It's all about our compassion!*

L. H.

*Beloved, rejoice with those who rejoice,
weep with those who weep.*

Romans 12:15

Time is filled with swift transitions.
Naught of earth unmoved can stand.
Build your hopes on things eternal.
Hold to God's unchanging hand.[1]

This great hymn of the church took on new meaning for me when my youngest son was in full kidney failure, awaiting his first dialysis. Our daughter was in jail, awaiting arrangement, and we were raising a preteen grandson. It's from my very transparent experiences that I can write about life changes that were filled with great challenge! As we walked in and out of Grelon's hospital room, and as Mista Chuck and I stood in court before a judge to explain that we would not be putting up bail for our daughter, Grian, to be released, the only thing that held us secure, sober, and sane was the reality that God's Word has stood the test of time.

Our rapid "transitions" were new to us, but they were not new to God. Our only hope and help was in holding onto God's unchanging hand and every promise contained in God's Word. Because of the practice of the spiritual disciplines, we have survived multiple series of "swift transitions"! And the people of God have surrounded us during each one of them. However, we have had to find ways to encourage ourselves along the way.

The spiritual disciplines of reading scripture, prayer, meditation, worship, and fasting liberate us from being destroyed by those "swift transitions" that fill us with fear, despair, and anger that we have no control over life! Whether we choose to do a private devotion using devotional materials such as *The Upper Room* or *Daily Bread*, whether we are devout Sunday school or midweek Bible study participants, or whether we participate in a lunch group meeting, reading scripture will lead us to a more authentic inward and spiritual attitude. This all equates to our continuing abilities to keep clicking along on all of our spiritual cylinders and growing despite our journey through pain.

When this series of swift transitions began, outside of the church that I served was a banner that caused traffic to slow down: "Advent Means Mary Is Pregnant! We Should Be Too!" Advent has always been my favorite season of the year, for the whole world has to stop and pay homage to the role of Mary, the mother of our Savior! I'd seen this sign years before at Wheaton UMC in Evanston and it had certainly had an impact on me. But I never thought that any "spiritual pregnancy" would be so painful, messy, and public. Yet, like Mary, I had to realize that giving birth demands stretching, wrestling, and much discomfort as well as pain.

I am convinced that God utilized my weekly news column, which follows the International Sunday School Lesson's "memory verse," and completing a publisher's deadline for *Trumpet In Zion, Year B*, to help me keep my sanity! Otherwise, I would never have picked up my Bible, and there were many days when I could not pray. Thank God for the laments of David in the Psalms. They prayed for me! And thank God for compassionate people who reached out to us and kept us in their prayers on the days when we could not formulate any!

My editor, Kim Martin Sadler, had asked me to write for her book, *The Book of Daily Prayer: Morning and Evening*. It's a book that followed the revised lectionary. Therefore, using the lectionary as my morning meditation gave me hope in seemingly hopeless times.

Years ago, as a first-year student at Garrett-Evangelical Theological Seminary I had become familiar with the lectionary and thought it was too "contrived." Still, I began to purchase *The United Methodist Music and Worship Planner* for its convenience of having an Old Testament, psalm, epistle, and Synoptic Gospel (Matthew, Mark, Like, and John) passage all on the same page.

The Hebrew text gave me a history of people who lived through swift transitions. The Psalms helped me to verbalize my prayers, as "the deer panted for the waterbrooks, so panted my soul for God" (Ps. 42:1 KJV). The epistles showed me how I was to look and to live as a follower of the Way. And the Gospel passage allowed me to walk with Jesus as he ministered despite the multiple transitions in his life. The beauty of the lectionary is that the stories of many women, although not preached about from pulpits, are included. Daily I discovered new truth for my life.

Soon the weekly scriptures began to inform my life, my journey with Christ, and my daily walk to represent God in the world. I discovered that the Holy Spirit began *speaking to me,* even before I could discover a passage to preach to the congregation on Sunday morning! As a matter of fact, the congregation was fed out of my overflowing bounty. The first word of hope always came to help me not get stuck in a place called down.

As life's swift transitions began to wreak havoc in our life, I began to diligently search the scriptures for answers, for guidance, and for counsel. Mista Chuck and I could find comfort in the promises of God as he prayed before we walked out of the door. We were more challenged than ever before to live our faith in the world, among doctors, nurses, technicians, attorneys, judges, other prisoners, bail-bonds persons, and bailiffs. I discovered that the lectionary was not confined to the sanctuary! It had to hold us up and hold us together in the midst of multiple storms. And I was fed enough to offer bread for the journey to others, wherever we might be during the day.

"Do everything without complaining or arguing, so that you may become blameless and pure, children of God without fault in a crooked and depraved generation, in which you shine like stars in the universe as you hold out the word of life" (Phil. 2:14–16). The Christian year begins with Advent and a blameless and pure virgin's story. In the midst of a "crooked and depraved generation," Christmas comes, again and again. It's a shining star in the universe that leads the wise to Jesus during Epiphany. And leading others to Christ is our sole purpose!

The season of Lent takes us on the journey with Jesus to the cross. There we discover the "Christ method" of dealing with the swift transitions. He surrounded himself with a community. He shared with them the Word, in parables, in stories, and from memory. He challenged them to become their best. He role-modeled for them. He sent them out, two by two. He became a mother and washed their feet. He became a father and hosted them at table. He became the Bread and the Wine, with thanksgiving. He died. And he rose again to bring us the Easter season! Then he showed himself to them and commanded them to wait for Pentecost.

With much prayer, meditation, and contemplation, the scared group waited together. On the day of Pentecost, the Holy Spirit came in, kissing, touching, imparting new life, new hope, and new power. The church was born and the church's "ordinary season of walking in the footsteps of Christ began. Those "swift transitions" were par for the course!

One year three United Methodist female clergy and a Lutheran female clergy met each Monday morning for lectionary studies. Our various life experiences, our different congregations, and our distinct worldviews allowed us to approach the scriptures with great expectations. Our congregations benefited from our "cross pollination," and we grew both individually and corporately.

Today, this experience continues in my workplace. Women from different walks of life gather with me on Monday, after work. We take turns choosing different books, some fiction, some religious works. We spent months reading *Showing Mary* by Renita Weems.

Whatever book we read always leads us to the Bible and into conversations about ourselves and other struggling women. For we are women who want to know what God says about our lives. We close with prayer that Wisdom will enfold us and carry us through the rest of the week and allow us to be healers in every place that we go. We recognize that we are the twinkling stars that must shine in a world filled with swift transitions. We laugh with one another and we weep with one another.

Grelon has died and now rests in peace with God. Grian remains imprisoned. Giraurd is now a teenager in high school! And the Living Word continues to feed Mista Chuck and me and helps us to grow in ways never before imagined. "Beloved, rejoice with those who rejoice; weep with those who weep." May it always be so for us, is my prayer!

Beloved's Personal Journal

We are not responsible for the actions of others. We are not charged with the mandate of transforming the church. We are not held accountable for the work of the Holy Spirit. We are, however, to be open to the work of the Holy Spirit within us to be more Christ-like in our attitude and our action! Paul did not anticipate that we, mere flesh, could, would, or should try to accomplish the impossible. The challenge before us is to do all that is possible, in every situation, and to leave all consequences to God. We must utilize the spiritual disciplines at our disposal so that we will not yield to the multiple temptations around us for repaying evil. Vengeance belongs to God (Deut. 32:35). How wonderful it is to take a couple of steps backward!

1. When was the last time that you had to "overcome evil with good"?

2. What is your understanding of the Christian year?

3. Define the spiritual disciplines that are most transforming to you.

4. In the midst of tense times in your life, what is your usual response?

16

WOMEN: GOD MADE US SPECIAL!

Jesus wants us for Son beams!

L. H.

Beloved, live in harmony with one another;
do not be haughty, but associate with the lowly;
do not claim to be wiser than you are.

Romans 12:16

EVERY MARCH IS WOMEN'S HISTORY MONTH, MARCH 8 IS National Women's History Day, and I love to take significant opportunity to salute every one of my sisters, great and small, young and older! March has been deliberately set aside to have the nation pause and reflect upon, with great thanksgiving, the legacy and legion of God's women who have birthed and continue to birth new worlds. I pray that in March you, your local congregation, your social set, your family, and your work group take the time to pay homage to some great and special woman who has been the bridge for you to cross. In every era, in every area, and in every sphere of our nation, there are massive imprints left by women. March is the month when we spotlight the achievements of women and remind every woman that God created us to be special!

In his letters, Paul paused to honor all of the women who worked in harmony with him to spread the message of Jesus Christ. I know that there are many women continuing this work without any title, formal designation, or professional status. Mrs. Coretta Scott King, who obtained a graduate degree in violin and voice, was not allowed to work outside the home after marrying young Rev. Martin Luther King Jr. It was unthinkable to have a wife work. The man was financially responsible for the home. So Mrs. King gave in to the dictates of the day and lived to create harmony for her spouse, who caught hell in the world! What has impressed me and so many others across the world is that for almost forty years after his death, she continued to advocate for the least, the last, and the forgotten, with the same passion as her spouse, and she did it in the public eye.

Like many people, I sat up until almost two o'clock in the morning February 6, 2006, viewing the tape of the funeral of Mrs. Coretta Scott King on C-SPAN. (Wondered why it was not on BET all day? Did you?) For most of my adult life, I have watched Mrs. King give of herself to "the dream" named by her husband. I felt it was my duty to pay my last respects too. Surely, she had been part of the "family." Certainly, she had been black America's most celebrated "first lady" of the very first black family in America! I felt that she was similar to Jacqueline Kennedy in beauty, dress, demeanor, mannerisms, and rise to global fame. She was a special lady. God made her so.

My last personal glimpse of Mrs. King was at the inauguration services for Dr. Sujay Johnson-Cook when the latter became president of the Hampton Minister's Conference. (Sujay was one of the key people who presided over Mrs. King's funeral. She and Yolanda King have been friends since college.) Mrs. King had always been a "she-ro" to me, as she presented herself to the world with sterling character, southern charm, amazing grace, and regal dignity. No, I never met her to know her personally, never had a conversation with her face to face, nor do I have a personal note in my collection from "famous folk." But I knew her. At least, I knew the woman that she presented to us. I liked what she allowed us to view, although I know there was another side, another voice, and a whole different story to her life.

Mrs. Betty Shabazz, Mrs. Merlie Evans, and Mrs. Coretta Scott King were all members of the Civil Rights Era Widows Club, an "unofficial" club they established to maintain their sanity after the brutal deaths of each of their spouses for the sake of the movement for equality. Left as single women with children, they did not have an easy lot in life. Yet, they portrayed harmony even with those who had caused them massive doses of horrendous pain. They did it for the sakes of their husbands and for the forward movement of the rest of the world.

Historian Darlene Clark Hine has written of the "culture of dissemblance," whereby black women "created the appearance of openness . . . but actually shielded the truth of their lives . . . from their oppressors."[1] Oh, what a powerful truth this is that I know quite well from personal experience. Sitting with a group of white sisters over soup one week, being the only woman of color present, I was asked if I had "energy" to do one more project calling the whole sisterhood together. I felt free enough to answer, "After awhile the white sisterhood becomes overpowering to me. I get tired of having to represent the black nation, answer for all the sistas, hold the opinions of every black woman, and accept the blame for all that is wrong." I know that I'm special. And I know that it's a burden to be born. Sometimes I am able to take off my "Superwoman cape." I'm making serious attempts to burn it up! But we never saw Mrs. King without her "cape." Her children, her advisors, and her wisdom counsel kept her wrapped in it until the bitter end.

It was my intent to salute women every month, not only in March. I didn't have a clue that my first role model for this work would be Mrs. Coretta Scott King. I was sad to learn that she actually died from the effects of an internal cancer in her reproductive organs that had been kept "secret" from the world. We didn't get the chance to pray for that specific affliction, although the family sought our prayers when she had the major stroke. Is there something shameful about speaking the word "uterus" in public? Is there yet the speculation that cancer in the uterus indicates a "sex life" or the lack thereof?

Mrs. King's daughter, Rev. Dr. Bernice King, preached a fascinating message about her mother's reproductive organs being attacked by the growing cancer that began to shut down other major organs in her body. She said that since Mrs. King had helped to "birth" the civil rights movement and held it so close to her heart, the hideous cancer of growing racism was shutting down all that she and Dr. King and Mrs. Rosa Parks lived and died for in the first place! You ought to hear the eulogy, for it was a powerful and wise revelation of the state of our nation, even the world.

The apostle Paul calls for us to live in and to live as God's creation, in harmony with all. The psalmist says: "Who are we, humans, that God is mindful of us? The offspring of humans, clay-dirt, that God cares for us? We have been made a little lower than the heavenly beings and crowned with glory and honor" (Ps. 8:4–5, my paraphrase). Dr. Eugene Peterson's *The Message* puts it like this: "God . . . why do you bother with us? Why take a second look our way? Yet we've so narrowly missed being gods, bright with Eden's dawn light. You put us in charge of your hand-crafted world, repeated to us your Genesis-charge, made us lords of sheep and cattle, even animals out in the wild, . . . God, brilliant Lord, your name echoes around the world" (Ps. 8:4–9). This is the Word of God, for the people of God, and Mrs. Coretta Scott King lived it from her heart! Thanks be to God for her role modeling and legacy.

The Rev. Dr. Safiyah Fosua, director of Invitational Preaching Ministries at the General Board of Discipleship for the United Methodist Church in Nashville, Tennessee, honors Mrs. King with this poem:

Remembering Coretta Scott King
April 27, 1927–January 30, 2006

O Lord.
The saints are marching in
Martin and Rosa
. . . now Coretta.

Who will stand in her place before you
Willing to give up her own dream
Of a home in the suburbs
And undisturbed summer nights
Without death threats and anonymous haters on the phone?
Who will take his place before you
Ready to struggle for your dream
Of a day when all of humanity loves like family
And none are set-aside for slave or lackey?
Now that the saints have begun to march in
Will we be overcome with nostalgia over days gone by?
Or will we continue to go forward?

On this day, when the bell tolls for Coretta Scott King
We give you thanks that
    there was once a woman who heard a word from you
        while kneeling alongside the man she loved
    we shared space with a woman who continued to carry out
    your vision
        even after it claimed her husband
    we felt the presence of an elegant woman who stood for God
        with the prophetic mantle draped around her shoulders.

Lord, may memories of
Coretta's life and Martin's life
Trigger
A renaissance of care, concern, and continued action
For the *least of these*
who continue to live among us.

Amen.[2]

May our lives, every special woman of God, honor both God and Mrs. Coretta Scott King in significant, lasting and life-changing ways. Remember to call, stop by and see, or send a card to a "special woman" who has invested in your life. It's the very least that we can do! "Beloved, live in harmony with one another; do not be haughty, but associate with the lowly; do not claim to be wiser than you are."

Beloved's Personal Journal

Harmony is not an easy concept to describe. Harmony is not an easy state to maintain. The apostle Paul gives us realistic and practical instructions about how to avoid disharmony in our relationships. All of his arguments are topsy-turvey to the way of the world. We know, as human beings, how to "get even," how to exact revenge and cause others to "pay back" deed for deed. We do not belong to the "world," however; our citizenship is in eternity. Contention in the body of Christ can become the crux of rising evil. Therefore, Paul is forthright in his command that we "repay no one evil for evil." The call for each of us is to seek the power of the Holy Spirit, who leads us to seek the ways that will lead to harmony.

1. How does your city, state, and congregation honor women in March?

2. What do you do as an individual to lift up the deeds of other women?

3. In what ways have older women influenced your life?

4. How would you describe the "harmony" in your life?

17

W E   A R E   F A M I L Y

❧ ❦

*The use of life's best practices for loving justice
and practical salvation is ours!*

L. H.

*Beloved, do not repay anyone evil for evil,
but take thought of what is noble in the sight of all.*

Romans 12:17

❧ ❦

"HISTORY, LIVED, NOT WRITTEN, IS SUCH A THING NOT TO understand always, but to marvel over. Time is so forever that life has many instances when you can say 'Once upon a time' thousands of times in one life."[1] So begins the marvelous, delightful, enchanting, and intriguing book *Family* by J. California Cooper. It is the story told of our origins, and of our beginnings in America, the land of the free and the home of the slave! It is the raw, gritty tale of a woman's existence in slavery. It grips the heart. It stimulates the mind. It draws the spirit. And it's so contemporary that it hurts!

J. California Cooper's description of darkness, pain, and severe struggles of a family speaks well for the endless days of journey that the children of Israel faced in the wilderness. We can try to spiritualize it as much as we want, but that could not have been an easy period in their lives. For none of us likes transition! We feel as if we are walking, working, and operating in a fog. The songwriter says it well, "You've got me going in circles.

Round and round I go."[2] It's a new name for the same day, over and over again.

And the people rebelled! They said to one another, "Let us make a captain, and let us return into Egypt." God had done marvelous things for them. God had worked miracles on their behalf. God had opened the Red Sea and allowed the horses and riders of their oppressors to drown in all the water they could not drink! God was leading them, guiding them with cloud and fire, assuring them they were not alone. God was raining down angels' food, manna. And when the people complained about not having meat, God sent them quails.

Their robes didn't wear out. Their sandals didn't run over or fall apart! They had it made. If, that is, you like being out in the middle of nowhere, with no promised land with houses and gardens in sight! God had the plan. Moses had a clue of the vision. But the people rebelled and wanted to go back to Egypt. I wonder how they thought they could swim across all that Red Sea. Or perhaps they felt that since they had made an executive decision, God would do a reverse miracle just for them. Like us, they were angry, scared, and not ready to "live in peace" but to take some action, even the wrong action.

They were headed forward with God and decided to go backwards by themselves. Sometimes I feel that we are living in the same time period! So, just as J. California Cooper wrote in her book, I too would wonder where those who had run off to seek freedom had gone. I too would sometimes just stand and squint my eyes at the stars in the sky, looking left and right in an effort to guess which way was north or whatever way was freedom. "But the sky is so big and endless, like time."[3] What does it take for us to do the noble or the right thing when it looks and feels like chaos all around?

The people could not believe God! They were so convinced of their doom and failure that they could conceive of being free. They saw themselves as small, minor, and insignificant to both themselves and to God! When Moses sent spies to check out the promised land, they brought up an evil report of the land they had searched, saying, "The land that we have gone through as spies is a land that devours its inhabitants; and all the people that we saw in it are of great size" (Num. 13:32). They are really, really big! They are most certainly our superior! They possess so much that they are the really big dominant culture! They won't give us those houses, those vineyards, and those rich, vast, lush, and fertile fields! So what that God performed all those miracles yesterday, even parting the Red Sea. That doesn't mean we can whip those big folks! So the Israelites formed a party of rebellion. And God got good and angry! Well, I don't think that rebellion is what the apostle Paul has in mind for us, today. For it got the children of Israel in deep trouble!

Whenever we forget who ordained our very existence and brought us thus far along the way, we are going backwards. When we fail to consider the provisions, the miracles, and the endurance that undergirds our very "isness," our very being, I'm persuaded that we are making God good and angry. When we refuse to see the land of opportunity and are afraid to snatch and seize what good things are before us, then we, like the children of Israel, are rebelling against the God who made us. God has made every provision when we decide to move forward, by faith. The way of the world, the way of the culture, and the way of the naysayers did not work before for God's people, and it won't work now! We have to be willing to trust God and to obey, knowing that God will take care of us, even when we can't "see" the way. We are called to walk by faith.

It's time for us to stop believing all of the world's evil reports. I don't care what research group gathered them. It's time for you and for me to cease being "media muppets," reading, believing, internalizing, and quoting all the bad stuff that is said about us in printed evil reports. Someone is always pulling the strings, calling the shots, and dictating what is viewed by us. There is no "real" news. What we get is always filtered according to some purpose unknown to us.

We have to learn how to have interior dialogues with our inner selves, our very best selves. We have to do the spiritual disciplines required to meditate, pray, hear God's still, small voice, and allow the power of the Holy Spirit to speak peace and truth in our very souls. "None of the people who have seen my glory and the signs that I did in Egypt and in the wilderness, and yet have tested me these ten times and have not obeyed my voice, shall see the land that I swore to give to their ancestors; none of those who despised me shall see it" (Num. 14:22–23).

"Time, time and life; they move on. History does not repeat itself, people repeat themselves"[4] For we are Family! "So, Beloved, do not repay anyone evil for evil, but take thought of what is noble in the sight of all."

Beloved's Personal Journal

Maybe you've been done wrong. Maybe you've been kicked when you were down, pushed aside, given no privileges and chances in life that you didn't have to scrabble for. Maybe it was even someone in your birth family or church family who hurt you. But Paul is saying we all need to move on! We know, as human beings, how to "get even," how to exact revenge and cause others to "pay back" deed for deed. We do not belong to the "world," however; our citizenship is in eternity. Contention in the body of Christ can become the crux of rising evil. Therefore, Paul is forthright in his command that we "repay no one evil for evil." As Christians, we are not to seek payback, but we are to take the proverbial "high road." Don't stoop to the level of those who hurt you, but rise above. You can't heal from your wounds until you forgive. And, hard as it may seem, you can do this through the power of the Holy Spirit.

1. What does family mean to you?

2. Have you ever given up on God and wanted to do things your own way?

3. If you are not in relation with someone in your family, pray and ask God to show you a way to heal that broken relationship.

4. Are there people in your birth or church family you need to forgive? Do you need to ask forgiveness from someone you have hurt?

5. The next time you read a negative statistic about your people, write down all of the positive things that you know people are doing in your church and/or community that never get in the news.

18

A CALL TO REMEMBER

Sometimes it is best to move away
when peace is absent and you are in peril!

L. H.

Beloved, if it is possible, so far as it depends upon you,
live peaceably with all.

Romans 12:18

I REALLY DO THINK I'M PRETTY SMART! I'M A VORACIOUS reader and have been all of my life. Somebody told me years ago that all types of secrets are hidden between the covers of books and that was the reason slaves were not taught to read. So ever since I learned how to read I've been discovering those secrets and sharing them with anyone who had a need to know. Television has never been too interesting to me. I can do a good movie every now and then, but TV has too many commercials and now too many swear words. So I basically stick to books. But, since I'm part of a family and a big screen television sits in our family room, the one television show I will partake in is *Wheel of Fortune*. The one I will not tangle with is *Jeopardy!*

Jeopardy requires me to remember too many facts. I don't understand how folks can become so filled with information that has virtually no meaning in real life. Most likely, the real reason I dislike this show is that it makes me feel dumb! I have a penchant to recall information—but not that much! As a person who has grown up in a dysfunctional family, I have made it a habit to remember details. When your every move is suspect, you begin to compile facts. As a writer, it's important that I can bridge information from the past and tie it to current events. But storing information in that computer called my mind is senseless to me. Random useless knowledge might win you big bucks, if you make it on a television show that requires such knowledge. There are some essential truths, however, that most of us tend to forget but that are well worth remembering.

As God calls people to faithful living, there were some basic facts that needed to be established. The first fact engraved on the hearts and minds of these former slaves, the Israelites, was: "I am the Lord your God, who brought you out of Egypt, out of the house of slavery; you shall have no other gods before me." This memory verse, found in Deuteronomy 5:6–7, is the first of the Ten Commandments. These former slaves had been delivered. They had been set free from bondage in a land where they were forced to make bricks without straw. The oppression had been so severe that they had cried out to God for relief. And relief was granted. God wanted them to remember who had been their Deliverer! It wasn't Moses. It was God.

The call to God's people was to remember. Remember who remembered you. Remember who came to your aid. Remember who was concerned for you. Remember who performed miracles on your behalf. Remember who has your back. Remember who is providing you with food and fresh water. Remember who is on your side! God is saying, "Don't forget. Remember." But the people of Israel forgot!

For months, then years, they wandered around in the wilderness, camping by Mount Sinai. While they were there, God wrote rules of life, codes of conduct, and lessons for survival. These rules were called the Ten Commandments. God wrote the Ten Commandments on tablets of stone and sent them back, inscribed, to the people. The people had said they wanted freedom. They had walked away from years of enslavement and captivity.

But they had forgotten who brought them out. They forgot God and enslaved themselves again in freedom!

Whatever you do, don't forget God. It doesn't matter what type of bondage you were in; God brought you out! There are no grades or levels of sin. All sin is sin! And sin is bondage to a god with a small letter "g"! Some of our gods are smaller than others. But they still keep us oppressed, tied up, chained to habits and substances we cannot break free from. Yet God delivers. God hears our cries for freedom.

I read the book "Not to People Like Us": Hidden Abuse In Upscale Marriages by Susan Weitzman, PhD.[1] The book is divided into four distinct sections for easy access for professionals and lay people to understand. Dr. Weitzman includes many charts, references, resources, copious end notes and worksheets for any of us ready to tackle this issue. The term "upscale violence" caught and held my attention. It indicates that there is an underserved population needing, desiring, and requiring our attention as we work to halt the established and escalating violence toward women and children in our world. Practicing psychotherapist Susan Weitzman, PhD, a lecturer at the University of Chicago's School of Social Service Administration, has done an extensive and intensive study of highly educated professional women who are snared in the throes of violence and secrecy. This is a must read for all of us who are working towards peace in our lives.

The back cover copy reads: "How is it possible for a highly educated woman with a career and resources of her own to stay in a marriage with an abusive husband? How can a man be considered a pillar of his community and regularly give his wife a black eye? The very nature of these questions proves how convinced we are that domestic violence is restricted to those who live at the lower end of the economic ladder. Now Dr. Weitzman explores a heretofore overlooked population of battered wives—the highly educated and upper income women who rarely report abuse and remain trapped by their own silence. Weitzman draws on her in-depth study of battered women to unveil the unique path taken by the upscale wife—the early warning signs, the internal dilemmas and decisions, and the dangerous desire to cover up abuse just to maintain appearances. Delving into the stories of wives and girlfriends, Dr. Weitzman offers critical information to help all women find their way out of abusive relationships and toward safety and independence.

A girlfriend of mine, Rev. Dr. Janette Chandler-Kotey, saw this book while shopping for groceries. She bought it for me and signed it with these words, "It's not just us, is it?" For the face of the abused that we see on the television screen is usually a person of color who is obviously poor and not well educated. This book, however, takes a qualitative study to show the high percentage of very wealthy women who endure, accept, and keep secret their abuse. What was awful was the way that we who work diligently on behalf of the poor seem to dismiss and to utterly disregard the plight of this upscale group, thinking that "surely it cannot happen to them"!

It was in the 1970s that explanations of wife abuse took on a feminist perspective. A 1976 *Ms.* magazine article made it clear that wife beating was occurring to the "woman next door." In 1979, *Violence Against Wives*, by Rebecca Emerson Dobash and Russell Dobash, professors in the School of Social Work and Social Policy at the University of Manchester, argued that marriage was an institution based on the subordination of women and that wife beating was an extension of male dominance and control. In this work, the authors discussed the power of myth in disguising wife abuse.[2] The myth is that it doesn't happen to the rich and the powerful.

The Faith/Trust Institute, founded by Rev. Dr. Marie Fortune, has presented one of the most impressive treatments of answering the "Why does she stay?" question. A woman sat in a chair covered with seven sets of sheets enshrouding her in the deep darkness of traditions, culture, institutions, patriarchy, religion, family customs, and sacred beliefs. For this woman of wealth, however, we have to face the reality that she has an additional layer for us to now consider. Her spouse's economic status in the community makes him a paragon of virtue! She is thus less likely to be believed by either her family or the authorities. He is more likely not to be held accountable for his actions and/or he will pay his way through the legal system.

A great benefit to Dr. Weitzman's work was the direct testimony of women who met over time and allowed their conversations to be transcribed. "Lynne," a law student, explained her reason for keeping her silence. "It's a class thing . . . I didn't know anybody that this happened to. I had kind of an elitist belief that it didn't happen to women like me—you know, professional women living on the North Shore [Chicago area]. It happens to a client, but it doesn't happen to us. I knew about clients who had been abused. A couple of them were homeless; a couple of them were on public aid. But I didn't know any women in my situation who where emotionally abused."[3]

Dr. Weitzman closes with these words that I echo wholeheartedly: "I hope this work beckons to these women, like the song from the old children's game: 'Come out, come out, wherever you are . . .' You are not alone."[4]

I we will just remember the freeing, liberating relationship with the One who loves us best, it will help us to stay free indeed. You might not ever make it as a contestant on *Jeopardy*, but this is not a bit of trivia you want to forget! "Beloved, if it is possible, so far as it depends upon you, live peaceably with all." And when there is no peace, Sweet Honey in the Rock sings, "Run . . . to a shelter"![5]

Beloved's Personal Journal

It is easier to live in peace with those you love and who love you than with people who are strangers, right?—or is it? Women are being abused every day by those they love and who say they love them. Even if we are not being abused, when we have problems sometimes it is just too easy for us to lash out at those who are closest to us, to take our stress out on those we care about. We can't usually control what others do. But we can control what we do and how we react to what others do. "As far as it depends on you," live in peace. This may be one of the hardest things God asks of us, but the power of God's Spirit is there to help us do the best thing.

1. Recall a serious situation that God brought you through. How did you respond to God's blessing?

2. List the Ten Commandments. Do you live by them?

3. How might these commandments strengthen you as a person?

4. If you or someone you know is suffering from domestic violence, make the decision right now to seek help. Remember, abuse can be psychological and emotional as well as physical.

19

YOU CAN'T BUY THIS

Take your hands, your mind, and your mouth
off the situation. Stop rewinding those old tapes!
Place it all in God's hands.

L. H.

Beloved, never avenge yourselves,
but leave room for the wrath of God; for it is written,
"Vengeance is mine, I will repay," says God.

Romans 12:19

THE ADVERTISERS REALLY DO THINK THAT THEY KNOW HOW TO get our attention. They hire folks with marketing skills and strategies to target our minds, our sense of self, and our wallets. They are acutely aware of what we "think" we deserve. They know how to package things, couch their pitch in just the right language, and flaunt it in our faces, whether the medium is television, radio, newspapers, magazines, mail service, e-mail, pop-ups, or billboards. Marketers are smart enough to know what it is that we really, really want. And they intend for us to buy it from their client. They know "us" because they know what it is that "they" also desire!

The advertisers come after select audiences with the goods most of us want to purchase but can't actually afford. They come with lures for our eyes, our emotions, and our desires for bigger, better, and more convenient things. Cigarettes, beer, and alcohol are not tasty items. Yet they are advertised all over racial ethnic neighborhoods, since they provide cheap thrills. Far too often than I like to admit, my personal downfall is the lure of the numerous financial options to purchase anything with cash, credit card, lease options, or that infamous lay-away plan! The ads tell us that for whatever we want, there is a method to purchase it!

I have to confess that I enjoy the ability to purchase the things that I like. "Stuff and things" are some of my favorite possessions. Sometime ago, we were traveling in a small town in Texas. We decided to see the sights by walking in the downtown area. There was a crystal bowl and vase in the window that caught my eye. Mista Chuck said, "Lynn, we can't get that fragile stuff home." Into the store I walked. Out of the store I came with a lay-away ticket and the promise from the owner to safely pack and ship my items.

They sure did arrive securely and are housed in one of my curio cabinets today. It oughta be called a "curiosity cabinet"! Now I'm curious as to just why I felt that I had to have those things on that particular day! And, truth be told, I bought them simply because I could. They have seldom been used. They sit and collect dust in a living room that we have to remember to visit! But, that day, I had buying power.

I have learned, however, that having the power to purchase is not the same as the power of knowing what is necessary and what is excessive! I tend to lean towards the excess. Being born African American in a time when black people were underpaid and not welcomed in most stores, I learned at a very early age the meaning of "can't afford." As the oldest of eight children with a father who did not "allow" my mother to work outside our home, many things were out of our reach. My mother's standard reply was "we can't afford that." I knew exactly what she meant. No other words were necessary and there would be no further explanation.

What began to sprout up within me was the express purpose of getting enough education and finding the right job that would allow me to afford anything that I wanted. I never thought of this as a trick of the enemy of my soul. I never realized that this little thought planted in the back of my mind would one day drive me to spend what I could not pay for with ready cash. I never thought that I would become enslaved to creditors because I wanted to have more than my parents could ever afford.

What I didn't factor in to my childhood determination was the habit of saving until I could afford to make my purchase. Nor did I see the necessity of "delayed gratification." Nobody ever taught me that the purchase of land was one of the best investments in the world. Although my parents owned a home, we never had a dinner table conversation about the ability of black people to buy land, to develop it, and to hold onto it as a legacy. There was so much economic "miseducation" that I lacked.

Our family did not discuss stocks and bonds. We only had Christmas Club accounts and saving bonds. When I was growing up, I didn't know about annuities and diversified portfolios. We did buy life insurance policies that grew in value. And my grandparents had both a savings account and a Christmas Club account; but no one invested in stocks.

Some of us take this "buying" thing even a bit further. We try to buy our way into areas that are restricted. We go overboard trying to impress the Smiths and surpass the Joneses. So we find ourselves believing and practicing the hype of the marketing geniuses. Many of us actually believe that we can "buy" our salvation, buy forgiveness, and even buy vengeance! But the time has come to realize that our money can only take us so far. God has no need or desire for what we can purchase.

We want our jobs, our titles, and our positions to carry weight in God's realm. We want people to recognize who we are by what we possess materially, while the real deal is that money does not count with God! God gives us jobs to make the medium of exchange for goods and services. But there is not going to be an ATM or American Express card in heaven!

Jesus entered the Temple and discovered those folks who sold as well as those who bought (Mark 11:15–17). The Hebrew Law had already established that those with little substance were to bring their sacrifice of a little dove. Those who had some substance were to bring a sheep as their sacrifice. Those who had amassed a great deal had to offer a bull as their offering. So there was a good reason for the animals to be in God's house. This was not the reason why Jesus turned over tables and chased folks out of the building. It had become such a trite ritual that those who were selling and those who were buying both felt that with a monetary exchange they were once again in harmony with God! Jesus looked at the deceived ones and essentially declared, "You can't buy your way to God!"

Little sin, medium sin, or large sin all count in God's realm. And the blood of Jesus is what covers our sin, only the blood of God's innocent Lamb. This occurred just a few days before the Passover, which commemorated the ancient memory of the Jews that death had "passed over" them, while taking the first born of all their enemies. Who was preparing to become the Passover? And what buyer or seller in the Temple could afford one splinter of the tree upon which the Christ of Glory was about to be hung?

From his actions, I dare say that empty ritual of buying "stuff" in God's house in God's name really ticked Jesus off! The meek, mild-mannered Jesus who had just endured the false hypocrisy of a triumphal entry into Jerusalem (Mark 11:1–9) was changed into a vicious driving force because the sacred place had become "cheap" to too many! God's Temple "is called a house of prayer for all nations" (Mark 11:17). It cost Jesus his life in order to pay for our "free salvation!"

What a challenge to chew on. For our lifestyles speak truly to the reality that we don't have it all together. We cannot purchase forgiveness, nor can we buy vengeance! Paul wants us to really think about the fact that all of life is in God's capable hands. What people do to us is too often not about us! It's about a pain, a sickness or a disease that is within them! So, they have really taken out their frustrations upon us, but not really because of us. This fact sinking into our reality will help us to move on from wanting payback. Honestly, we are not that important to that many people!

We need to back up and to reframe, rethink that issue, that situation that has us in such a tight squeeze. Think about what might have been going on with people who have done you wrong to make them behave in such an ugly manner. Begin to see their lives through their eyes. It becomes easier to pray for them. It becomes easier to let go of the need to repay a hurting individual. It does not excuse what they did. But it makes it much easier for you to ask the Savior to help you work through to release.

What we discover as we walk the talk of salvation is that too many times we hurt others too! The reality is that none of us has it all together. There are many days when we cause others much pain. When we ask God for forgiveness, if we will forgive the one who hurts us, our slate is wiped clean. When we withhold forgiveness, God cannot and will not forgive us either. When it comes down to this, we can be relieved that even when none of us have it all together, thanks be to Jesus Christ, in community we do have it all! "Beloved, never avenge yourselves, but leave room for the wrath of God; for it is written, 'Vengeance is mine, I will repay,' says God."

Beloved's Personal Journal

What a blessing to know that without any purchase price on our behalf, we can be given access to the Holy of Holies when we forgive others and stay in right relationship with God. Healing comes with forgiveness. No matter who we are or think we are, we can't see the big picture—but God can see our tomorrows. Paul instructs us to make sure our own house is in order and leave other peoples' messes up to them and God to deal with. What others intend for evil, God can turn to good, so we must forgive others and trust God for the outcome.

1. If you are financially illiterate, learn how to become financially astute. Begin reading business magazines and books that can help you to understand stocks and bonds and, more importantly, how to make your money grow.

2. List the things that you waste money on. For the next twelve months, eliminate wasting money on these things. Save the money in a savings account that you would have wasted. At

the end of the year, donate it to a women's shelter to help women who have far less than you.

3. Read Matthew 6:25–34. Scripture says that we should seek first God's realm and righteousness, and everything we need will be given to us. Before you think about spending money on yourself or wasting money, pray to God and ask God to bless you so that you can offer a part of your blessing to an organization or maybe start an organization that you have always wanted to start that will help those who are in great need.

20

IT TAKES A WOMAN TO BIRTH A VILLAGE

*Practice being love and watch God
so punish your enemies that you will begin
to pray for them!*

L. H.

*Beloved, if your enemies are hungry, feed them;
if they are thirsty, give them something to drink; for by doing
this you will heap burning coals on their heads.*

Romans 12:20

HAVE YOU EVER BEEN REJECTED? YOU KNOW WHAT I MEAN, a good, old-fashioned case of being deserted, abandoned, dropped, kicked to the curb, and "dissed"! The truth of the matter is that every one of us can quickly answer "Yes!" For it is not an uncommon occurrence to be dumped! As a matter of fact, it happens pretty regularly. You think things are going along fairly well when all of a sudden, out of the blue, the phone calls stop, the sweet talk ceases, and you find yourself not "cutting the mustard" for the person in question anymore. As James Ingram so sweetly sings, "I guess my best wasn't good enough!"[1] It's not a nice feeling. It's not a pleasant experience.

Being dumped is not an occasion we like to recall, reflect upon, or remember. If it's only happened to you once, can you imagine what it would feel like five times? What would be the size of the hole in your soul? How big would the gaping wound be that was forged by five uncaring, unkind, and insensitive husbands or significant others? A woman has had this awful experience and she has much to teach you and me!

The New King James Version of John 4:4 reads, "But he [Jesus] needed to go through Samaria." I so appreciate this reading. For this was no casual mishap, no incidental meeting, no midnight creep like the one pulled by Nicodemus. Jesus was intentional and deliberate; he made a calculated decision about going to Samaria and keeping a date with a hurting woman when neither the day nor her life was in its best state!

It was about noon. It was a hot time in the woman's life. Most likely she felt that things couldn't get any hotter than they were. We find Jesus coming to see about a woman when it was hot! The scriptures go on to detail that "Jews have no dealings with Samaritans" (4:9). Yet Jesus stops at an old well, meets a hurting woman, asks her for a drink of water, and listens to her sassy response, "How is it that you, being a Jew, ask a drink from me, a Samaritan woman?" (4:9). Naturally, her first reaction had to be one of shock. Jesus went on to explain that he had living water he was offering her in exchange. It's living water that will spring up inside of us to renew us, refresh us, revive us, and slake our inner thirst. When Sister came to comprehend what Jesus meant, she asked to receive this gift. The girl was no dummy!

Then Jesus decided to address her hot issue. We have forty-two verses of record, which is the longest portion of dialogue between Jesus and any other person in all of the Synoptic Gospels. Just three verses deal with the woman's "six" husbands. The five who had divorced her and the one she was now living with came into the picture. "Jesus said, . . . you have had five husbands and the one whom you now have is not your husband" (4:16–18). This is where we must stop, for we are not talking about a situation that happened recently.

This passage was written almost two thousand years ago when women were simply the property of their fathers until they were given over to become the property of their husbands. There was no courtship and choosing of a mate. The marriage makers negotiated with the parents to seal a marriage covenant. If the husband ever became dissatisfied (as often occurred when a male heir was not produced), a man was allowed to divorce, and, it was always the woman's fault! All he had to do was go to the gate, state his case before the male elders and get their decision to return to his tent, face the east, where Jerusalem's Temple was located, and declare three times, "I divorce thee." The woman was only permitted to take what he allowed as she returned to her father's house as soiled goods!

Five times Girlfriend had been bought and paid for. Five times she had high hopes, wishes, and desires that "this is the one." But five times she had been rejected. Was she in hot water or not? Jesus came to deal with her broken heart, crushed spirit, and feelings of low self-esteem. He did it by making it worse before it could be made better! For in telling her that the man she had now was not her husband, Jesus tied the sixth one to all the others who had done her wrong before.

Like us, she wanted someone to make her feel good about herself. She needed someone who would accept her for who she was. She had a romantic dream, perhaps a fantasy of a male who would care about her needs, be a friend and a companion. But instead, she kept getting men who ran off and left her with additional pain! Been there? Done that?

Now this woman is a prime example for the apostle Paul, who tells us to "feed our enemies, and to bring drink to the thirsty." For this sister is getting water to do the household chores for a man who is about to run her off again! Yet when Jesus encounters her about her relationships, notice that she never blames the man or the men in her life. When she is forced to face the victimization of her life, she stands tall and receives it as fact. There is no drama. There is no smart talk, quick answers, or comic remarks. She does not slam any man who has hurt her. She does not point fingers at her father, brothers, or family, but she stands and listens to the truth. All the while, the man, at home, is about to be dropped like a hot potato! In the stillness of this

moment, hot coals of fire are being put upon his head as she
stands in a growing spot of liberty and freedom. She is released
from taking that clown any water! So she leaves the water pot! I
applaud the sister!

I'm sick and tired of those preachers who try to make this
woman into some slut, whore, or sinner. The passages say nothing about these issues! We bring our own agendas to the passage
and twist what Jesus went to Samaria to do! He went to do pastoral care and inner healing to a sister who was in dire straits!
When we stop running to all those old familiar places, seeing the
same old familiar faces, doing the same old familiar things, Jesus
is waiting for us to offer refreshing, living water in order that we
might learn to love ourselves! When you love yourself, your standards change. When you love yourself, your attitude will change
and your actions as well. When you love yourself, your "attracting
antenna" will begin to draw a different sort of individual into
your world. Jesus is waiting on you and me to stop being our own
worst enemies.

After their meaningful and healing conversation, Girlfriend
left her water pot, ran into town, and let the town know that
there was a man by the well telling folks' business! At least five
men didn't want their selfish story put into the town news! The
Bible records that the whole town came and made the acquain-
tance of Jesus and asked him to stay for awhile. They did it because a formerly hurting woman had been touched and made
whole. She was never, ever the same! This is truly a wise woman's
story!

What I love most about this story is that the "boys" were not
there to try and crash the party. One year at the Hampton
Ministers' Conference, I heard Pastor Jackie McCullum remark
about this passage of scripture that since the disciples were not
able to handle the "new thing" that Jesus was about to do in the
earth, through a woman, he had sent them shopping! The "new
thing" that Jesus did, just in case you have not figured it out, was
to make a Gentile woman the very first evangelist! Even after the
resurrection, the boys didn't get it, but this woman had already

won souls to Jesus before the crucifixion! "Beloved, if your enemies are hungry, feed them; if they are thirsty, give them something to drink; for by doing this you will heap burning coals on their heads."

Beloved's Personal Journal

Jesus was so amazing in the fresh, new way he dealt with hurting people. Today we might say he really knew how to "think outside the box." His interaction with the Samaritan woman at the well not only met her need and brought the good news to a whole town, but it broke open, put a whole new slant on, and set an example for a new way of thinking about the role of women and the relationship between who is "in" and who is "not in." God's realm has room for all of God's people. If we "love our enemies, and pray for those who persecute" us, we can trust that the Holy Spirit will work good from our situation.

1. What type of person are you in a relationship? Are you the giver or the receiver? Are you the communicator or the complainer? Are you the needy one or the one who caters to others' needs?

2. Have you ever been rejected by someone whom you loved because you fit one of the personalities above? How did you handle the situation?

3. Jesus crossed the boundary when he spoke to the Samaritan woman. How might you begin a meaningful relationship with someone whom you would not normally speak to?

21

THE KING AND I!

*The winning strategy is to do random acts
of kindness often! Be light! Be love!*

L. H.

*Beloved, do not be overcome by evil,
but overcome evil with good.*

Romans 12: 21

AUGUST 28, 1963, WAS A DAY OF EXTREME PAIN, UPHEAVAL, AND life change for me. Not only is that day distinguished by the March on Washington, but it was the birthday of my youngest son, Grelon Renard Everett. My oldest son, Gregory Raymond Everett, and I had been sent home by my husband from California to be with my grandmother for this scary event. The evening before, all of us had sat in front of the television set to watch the coverage of preparations for the largest gathering of black folks in this nation's history. It was an event I really wanted to see, but my labor pains had begun!

My mother was the designated driver who was to take me to Methodist Hospital in Gary, Indiana, check me in, and sit with me in the labor cubicle. I don't know who was in the most pain, Mother or me. With every pain that I had, with every examination, as I moaned, Mom blanched. I couldn't stand watching her suffering! Finally around 4:00 A.M., I persuaded her to go home. The pains were not really increasing; birth was not imminent. At

115

7:00 A.M., I found my clothes, waddled down the hall and out the door, and got inside a waiting taxicab. The driver asked "Aren't you going in the wrong direction?"

Needless to say, my grandmother was surprised to see me! But since there were no televisions in the labor and delivery section at the hospital, I was determined to watch as much of the march as possible before being forced to return to the hospital. Of course, the pains increased in intensity! But I walked the floor with the television turned up loud. I was filled with immense pride to see such a vast gathering of people. They were orderly. They were well dressed. They were filled with great anticipation. The largest "church" service in my history was set to take place with a pastor-preacher who had a reputation for straight talk that would "wreck a house!"

I saw people whom I had only read or heard about. I was "there" at the Lincoln Memorial, in the crowd, part of our new and emerging history as a united people. The course of our journey in this country was changing. I wanted to see, to hear, and to experience the directions of our "drum major for freedom." The Rev. Dr. Martin Luther King Jr. spoke directly to me! Dr. King's speech touched my heart. His pathos and passion penetrated my spirit. His grasp of our history and his hope for our future took root in my mind. The dream hooked me. When Dr. King finished, I realized that I too had a dream!

My grandmother called Mama as the speech was drawing to a close around 5:00 P.M. "Come and get this gal back to the hospital before this baby is born on my floor!" As the car wheels turned, it was to the beat of "I have a dream." My counting as the pains came closer was to the rhythm of "I have a dream." There was no "check-in" at the hospital—my pains were too close. I remember Mama saying, "Anything you need to know about her, ask me." They took me straight to the delivery room, where every "push" was to the strength of "I have a dream." And a bit before 6:00 P.M., my son Grelon was born into the world hearing the words, "you are the dream and the hope of the slaves!" The King and I had a baby!

For the dream of Dr. King was not confined to him alone. His dream was only part of the vision of the "King" of the universe! Martin was clear in always saying, "I have a dream." Never did he declare that he had "the" dream. God has always dreamed a world of unity, community, and freedom where each one of us can achieve our fullest potential. One of the great theologians, Meister Eckhart, asked a great question in the fourteenth century: "What does God do all day?" Since it was a rhetorical question, he answered it himself: "God lies on a maternity bed, giving birth to dreams." Those dreams have always been part of God's universal psalm of shalom. God has always allowed "whosoever will" to have a dream! God has no respect of persons. Dreams come as thoughts, ideas, visions, and daydreams that are incomplete, untried, and untested. Any willing soul is able to become pregnant with a thought, allow it to take root in their being, become consumed by their part in the unfolding drama of eternity, and join the league of God's dreamers!

I want you, every reader, to know that a group of serious women gathered and we prayed for you! Women came in the midst of blowing, swirling, sticking snow to pray for all of our diverse needs so that we might not be overcome by the raging evil in the world. It was a deliberate, concentrated effort to bombard the throne room of glory and "just have a little talk with Jesus." There were veteran prayers and novices in attendance. There were young, middle-aged, and senior sisters present. There were professional women, unemployed women, and busy homemakers. There were crying women, screaming women, moaning women, laughing women, and rocking women gathered in that room. They sat. They stood. They folded their arms. They lifted their hands. They prayed silently. They prayed aloud. They said their prayers. They stumbled through their prayers. They read biblical prayers. They were so articulate and powerful in praying that bedlam broke out, lamenting was heard, and the demons were put on notice that they had to flee! This Convocation of Prayer was an act of love where sistas (and a couple of serious brothers) were surely on purpose as we prayed for dreamers!

Being an on-purpose dreamer means having a focus in your life and knowing how to center in on it. Being an on-purpose dreamer means that you know God has called you, chosen you to do a particular task in the earthly realm, and will provide you with backup at all times. Being an on-purpose dreamer means taking aim at a particular goal and being willing to work and wait until it is achieved. Being an on-purpose dreamer means having the ability to do what needs to be done, regardless of the loud acclaim or the silent dismissal by the world. Being an on-purpose dreamer means that you realize that you plus God are a winning majority! Being an on-purpose dreamer means you realize why God created you in the first place and you fully comprehend that no one else can replace you. Being an on-purpose dreamer puts joy in your soul and glide in your stride and gives you "the" reason for getting up every day and starting all over again!

Being an on-purpose dreamer requires spending quality time in prayer with God. It means getting to know yourself. It means being able to accept the good and the bad parts of your personality. It means being able to name and claim both your strengths and your weaknesses. It means being so well acquainted with yourself that you know what turns you on and what turns you off. To be an on-purpose dreamer demands that we know and operate within the areas of our spiritual gifts, which make us a blessing to the body of Christ. To be an on-purpose dreamer makes you a gift to those you touch. Being an on-purpose dreamer allows you to feel good about what you contribute and allows you to have less of that human tendency toward jealousy! It permits you to become an active cheerleader for others to get on purpose and to work out their dream!

Those awesome hours of prayer were purposeful, for the women who came knew within their hearts that God had called them to be intercessors for dreamers and activist. Intercession is more than praying for your own personal and family needs. An intercessor is one who is willing to stand in the gap for others (some they know, others they don't know) to pray when others cannot or will not. They will pray when others don't know how and will pray until God hears and lifts their burdens. Intercessors will hold onto the horns of God's altar when it seems as if all hell has broken out and there is no hope. Intercessors have a burden on their hearts for the lives of others and can't help it! They don't ask for the burdens, they just purpose in their hearts to follow God's plan for their lives. Intercession in prayer is a divine purpose.

I remember the very hour I first realized that being in fellowship with God gave me the right and the privilege to pray for folks across the world (as well as those in my house!) and gave me the assurance that God would intervene because of my intercession. AWESOME! Talk about purpose! A songwriter who recognized how important it is to be on purpose in prayer wrote: "Somebody prayed for me, had me on their mind, took the time to pray for me. . . . I'm so glad they prayed for me!"[1] We prayed for you! We are told in scripture, "whatever your hands find to do, do it as unto the Lord." Translated, it means do it with purpose! We took that verse literally and lifted you and your needs for your dreams in our prayer! There is a very special design for your life that will allow the body of Christ to further overcome evil with good.

Believe me, Mother Rosa Parks was a dreamer too. She had dreamed of riding on the bus, being able to sit wherever she chose. She had received this vision of fulfillment from beyond herself. For it had "always" been that colored people sat and stood in the rear. But her vision of sitting anywhere on any bus was a piece of God's bigger dream. Her dream connected with Dr. King's dream, and the rest is history! Yet these two were only a small part of the army of dreamers who came before them and those who have continued to follow their lead. The dream did not begin in either Montgomery or in Washington, D.C. The dream came from God, Ruler of the universe, Creator of the world. This is the "King" who gives dreams, motivates and encourages dreamers, and pulls others into its grasp. This "King" and I can allow Dr. Martin Luther King Jr. to rest in peace!

The world continues trying to bring Dr. King back! But if he could return, he wouldn't! The nation didn't give him wholehearted support while he was alive. He had more than his fair share of back-stabbers, Monday morning quarterbacks, and leaders who wanted to take his place at the front of the parade. Like most black preachers, he was overworked, overexposed, overburdened, and very much underpaid. Harry Belafonte helped to pay for his funeral and provided money for the family, along with a white brother who had got him a life insurance policy. Why would he come back? Look at how his so-called "friends" have written exposes, his alma mater has shamed his work, and today's retrenchment of hard won rights makes the dream look more like a nightmare. He wouldn't come back! He ran a good race. He finished his course. Let him rest in peace!

Not Dr. King, not Mrs. Parks, nor Mrs. Coretta Scott King need return to this earth. They have done their part to not be overcome by evil, but always overcome evil with their good. They have taught and role-modeled nonviolence and faithfulness unto God by their very lives. It's that other King, the ultimate Ruler, the soon coming Sovereign, who is in charge. God's dream is yet alive. Many other dreamers are working, doing their part to overcome evil with good, and God will connect all the pieces at the proper time. I continue to work diligently at fulfilling my piece of the dream. The King and I are in partnership. What about the King and you? "Beloved, do not be overcome by evil, but overcome evil with good."

Beloved's Personal Journal

We shall overcome! We have dreams to dream, and work to do! God is calling us to continue what Jesus ushered in, what the early church kept going, and what the Holy Spirit has nurtured over the centuries—bringing God's dream, God's realm into a messed-up, hurting world. Paul instructs us to overcome evil with good so God's dream can be a reality. And he has told us how to use our spiritual gifts to do it, so the body of Christ will function together with a united purpose. Let's work together, energized and directed by God's Holy Spirit, to make Gods' dream our dream, and to make it happen!

1. What is your dream? Have you fulfilled it yet? What plans have you made to realize your dreams?

2. If you don't have one already, start a prayer list. Put down the names of all those who have asked you to pray for them and those who have not. Pray for each person by calling out each one's name to God. Be their intercessor and believe that God will answer your prayers.

3. Step out on faith just like Rosa and Martin. Consider organizing a prayer group at work. Pray and ask God to send the people who will gather with you.

22

T H E   A F T E R W O R D

❧ ❧

It's Been a Long Time Coming,
But I Know a Change Is Gonna Come!
Sam Cooke

❧ ❧

THE SITUATION IS BAD. IT'S GETTING WORSE. THE CHILD IS OUT
of control; the behavior is increasingly bizarre. The doctor can't
name the cause, but the pain continues. The marriage is aging,
but intimacy is absent. The meetings are predictable, but community is not present. You're studying harder, but the grades don't
reflect it. You're talking less, but the arguments are increasing.
Communion is served and taken, but love, charity, and harmony
are not experienced. The job is there, but no security is felt.
Everywhere your life is unpredictable.

All control is gone. You've played your best hand. You're
powerless and you know it. There's no method or strategy working, regardless of how much effort you've employed. You're helpless. You profess it. Finally, you admit that your life is totally un-
manageable. You want to run away. But you can't. You want to
quit. But you don't dare. You want to give up. But, deep down
within you, there's a teeny-weeny, itsy-bitsy strain of hope.

From somewhere in the recesses of your mind an old tune
begins a journey to your spirit. From the ancient storage of your
memory the ballad starts to crawl and creep into your conscious-
ness. From the stored tapes of yesterday, you begin to literally

hear these familiar words of faith. "It's been a long time coming, but I know a change is gonna come."[1]

For in the midst of a world of trouble, in a time of perplexing distress, in your worst period of trial, tribulation, and trouble, the Holy Spirit will remind you to hold on to hang in there and don't give up—for help is on the way. The words of scripture come to comfort someone who is going through and has been for a long time. The words of faith come to offer hope and healing for someone who feels discouraged and thinks that God does not care. There is good news for the people of God who are hanging on solely by the hairs on their chinny-chin-chins. God knows how you feel and guarantees you that it may have been a long time coming, but change is gonna come.

Thank God for the present and powerful Holy Spirit, who comes as our paraclete, our companion, our reminder of the precious promises of Jesus Christ. It may come as a surprise to many, but the truth is that the Holy Spirit doesn't come to just make us jump, run, scream, cry, and shout. The purpose of the Holy Spirit is to remind us of what Jesus said. After the resurrection, just before he lifted in ascension to the heavens, he promised his followers, "In a little while you won't see me, but I'm going to send you a comforter. I've got to leave you, but in a little while, I'm going to send you a consoler. I can't remain with you in a physical body, but in a little while, I'm going to send you a helper who will never leave you or forsake you. You won't be able to see me, but in a little while the Holy Spirit will come to live inside of you. *I will never leave you or forsake you.* And, even when it feels like you're all alone and life seems to have you in a place called down and out, hang in there, hold on, don't give up. It's been a long time coming but you've got to stand still and know, a change is gonna come!"

This oldie but goody, written and performed by Sam Cooke in 1963, is a song of the civil rights era. It's a song written to people of color who have been enslaved in the land of the free and the home of the slave. It's a song written in memory of those folks who knew what it meant to work from sunup to sundown with no pay and little food. It's a song written for folks who watched their family members be sold, their loved ones killed, their community constantly destroyed, and their dreams for a peaceful promised land dashed over and over. It's a song for those who know about separate and unequal, those who are well acquainted with the back of the bus, the colored washrooms, and colored water fountains. It's a song for those who could cook the food and yet not be served at those restaurants. It's a song for those who could clean the rooms in big, spacious houses and never rent or own one in a decent part of town. It's a song of faith in a God who is faithful to every promise written in the book of record.

Regardless of how long you've been going through . . . makes no difference how painful the situation has been holding onto the anchors of your heart . . . despite the fact that it seems as if even Almighty God has forgotten your name, address, birthday, and social security number . . . in spite of the reality that you've fasted, prayed, touched, and agreed with seven prayer partners, been anointed with oil, slain in the Spirit, and fasted for three lunch hours . . . regardless, the devil wants you to believe that where you are is the end of the line. The enemy of our soul wants to trap you into feeling that this is the awful place designed to take you down. But you've got to know and you've got to know that you know—it's been a long time coming, but a change is gonna come.

A passage from the prophet Jeremiah (Jer. 29) is a story about faith in action. It's a story of hope in the very face of a long and horrible enslavement and confinement. The people of God were exiled to a foreign land. The church of God was sitting in a guarded retention camp, while Jerusalem has been captured and occupied by the Babylonians. In a time of trouble and tribulation, a word came from God. Jesus declared that "my sheep know my voice." In the midst of problematic circumstances, God will speak to you. In the very time of seemingly hopeless and alarming predicaments, God will speak. In the very eye of the whirling storm, with junk, debris, and all types of garbage being tossed to and fro in your life, God will speak.

For God is not silenced by our troubles. God does not hush because Satan is cutting the fool. God is not voiceless because there seems to be no way out. Friends, when you are going through, be on the alert, for God will speak.

"A Change Is Gonna Come" is a song of faith. It is a song of hope. It is a song about rocking steady and being determined not to give up. It is a song to encourage those who knew long, sleepless, tearful nights and days filled with gloom and cloudy skies. This song was a word of hope to stormy weather people, sitting in the midst of a torrential downpour of hatred and severe mistreatment. It was a song written to say, don't just watch the rain. In the midst of rain, thunder, and lightning, that is the time to stretch your neck and began to look for the rainbow. The song says do not allow situations to cause you to hang your head in hopelessness. While the devil is acting up, you began to look up in faith.

Even though it's been a long time since the Middle Passage and the auction blocks . . . although it's been a long time since plantations and "happy darkies" . . . despite that it's been a long time since Reconstruction and empty promises . . . notwithstanding that it's been a long time since civil rights were pledged and then reneged upon, time after time after time . . . even with all of this being our truth—nevertheless, our task is to hold on to the Living Word of God! In the midst of dire straits, difficult days, dwindling finances, messed-up relationships, and uncooperative folks both at home and on the job, if we hold on to the Truth of the God who never fails, if we keep faith in the God of yesterday, today, and tomorrow—it may have been a long time, but know this morning that change has got to come!

Jeremiah heard God clearly. Jeremiah understood that he was going to sound foolish. Jeremiah was sure that what God was commanding wouldn't make sense to all of the "church members," the Israelites who were sitting in captivity, faraway from their promised land. But when God spoke, Jeremiah wrote. When God spoke, Jeremiah purposed to call out this crazy plan laid down by God. When God spoke, Jeremiah provided the strategy for change to come their way.

"Thus says the Lord of hosts, the God of Israel, to all the exiles whom I have sent into exile from Jerusalem to Babylon: 1)

Build houses and live in them. Plant gardens and eat what they produce. 2) Take wives and husbands and have sons and daughters . . . that they may bear sons and daughters; multiply there and do not decrease. 3) But seek the welfare of the city where I have sent you into exile, and pray to God on its behalf, for in its welfare, you will find your welfare" (Jer. 29:4–7).

You've got to see the picture. Israel was a backsliding nation. Babylon had kicked their behinds once again. Their promised land had been taken away by foreign invaders. Their leadership had been rounded up, deported, and locked up in Babylon. Their homes had been confiscated. Their property had been divided among the conquerors. Their Temple had been desecrated. Jerusalem now lay in ruins. It looked like the church was down and out.

For forty long years, under five kings, Jeremiah had preached "repent or be doomed." For forty long years, this messenger of God had preached, but the people would not listen. For forty long years, Jeremiah had stood alone, weeping and wailing over the conditions of a backsliding child named Israel. Understand that Jeremiah was not a Bishop T. D. Jakes. No one wanted to hear him preach. Jeremiah was not a Bishop Paul Morton. People didn't flock to his Full Gospel Six-in-One conventions. Jeremiah was not a Creflow Dollar. He was considered a miserable failure by popular standards. Jeremiah never attained material success. He underwent severe deprivation. The old boys club turned on him, plucked out his beard, and threw him in a pit. His neighbors rejected him and the ministerial alliance wouldn't allow him membership. But Jeremiah was faithful to God. Jeremiah was committed to God. Jeremiah was courageous. Jeremiah was bodacious. And Jeremiah knew the voice of God. So he wrote to the people with a plan from God.

Essentially, God told the church to invest in a foreign land. "You are in exile. Don't expect quick deliverance and microwave escape! This is a situation you got yourself into by your own choices. Your current position is one that you earned due to your willful disobedience to the will of God. Now that you're in hot water, don't expect me to hurry up, come quick, get there right now, and fix the mess you're in. But I've got a plan for you while you're in the mess you made, to contribute to your own deliverance. While it feels like your heart is going to break, cooperate with the plan of action I've laid out. Take some risks even when you don't understand my thinking. For my ways are not your ways. My thoughts are not your thoughts." God does have the better and best idea.

We don't have to understand its logic. We don't need to be able to figure it out. But the plan is to stop whining, stop complaining, stop grumbling and mumbling, and do something different. Put something of yourself into the mess you've made. Invest in building up your own house. Stop tearing down what's not going right. Stop pulling apart what you don't like. Give something. Offer something. Invest where you are. Plant where you are. Cultivate where you are. God never promised to come to Babylon and fix their situation. Rather, God told them to work in the place they found themselves.

Your marriage isn't working? Invest in it. Take a class on communications and conflict resolution. Your children are acting crazy? Invest in them. Take an effective parenting class. Learn to listen. Is illness getting you down? Invest in speaking wellness to yourself. Stop claiming sickness. Begin to stretch your body, exercise your temple, and pamper yourself. Church ain't what you like? Speak out and offer suggestions. Find a need and offer to fill it. Come to administrative counsel and lend a hand. Is your school going crazy? Are teachers ignoring you? Invest in a computer class, learn more, impress them, and show them how much you will learn in spite of them. Is singleness getting to you? Invest in you. Network, mentor children who will love to see you and accept whatever you have to offer. The situation will not get any better until you really decide to go to work and invest yourself.

God says multiply. Are your children acting the fool? Plant what you have to offer into the lives of other children who appreciate and love you. Stop trying to buy your children's love. Invest what you have where ever it will be received. All children belong to us. We are all connected. You are not simply responsible for the children you brought into the world. Can't have a child? Invest in the ones who have no parent. Take a class. Start a group. Join a study club and improve your mind. Join an exercise program and invest in your health. Organize a group. Teach something that you specialize in and be blessed. For you have got to multiply. God has decreed that we have to increase and not decrease. If the folks around you won't accept your gifts, there are some folks who are crying out, praying, and asking God to send you their way. There are many captives who need what you have to invest.

People of God, we are in the right place, wherever we are! For the steps of the righteous are ordered by God. People of God, there is no spot where God is not! Even in the tough situation you're in right now. People of God, the strategy for getting out of a bad situation is laid out before us. It is God's plan. And we have to work this plan. Yes, it's been a long time coming, but a change is gonna come when we work God's plan. Wherever you are, God says seek the welfare of the place that you are in. Pray for the ones causing you pain. Pray for the ones causing you hurt. Pray for the very place you want to leave! Seek the welfare of the very place where you have been exiled, says God. It's not to be a prayer of curse and damnation. It's to be a prayer for blessing. The prayer is simple: God bless this situation. God bless this person. God bless this mess. God doesn't need your specifics. God doesn't need our directions. We have simply been commanded to pray for their welfare, their benefit, and their best good. It doesn't make sense. It doesn't seem fair. It doesn't feel just. But it's God plan.

For when we pray for the welfare of our captors, our enemies, and those who have done us wrong, God has promised that we will find our best good! When we pray for those who despitefully use us, God promises to intervene on our behalf. Folks, it's time to get busy. It is praying time!

Sista Linda, you might say, that sounds nice and biblical. But you don't know my situation. You couldn't possibly have a clue about the mess I'm going through. There is no way you can tell me that my problem is going to get better. I've done everything humanly possible. I've strategized, networked, organized, plotted, planned, cussed, fussed, fallen out, and decided to throw up my hands in disgust. There is no way something so simple can get me out of the place I'm in.

Friend, this passage of scripture comes at just this point in our lives. For our extremity is God's opportunity to show up and to show out. When we decide that God actually does know more than we do, we can follow the plan and sit back and wait for God to work. It's been a long time coming, but a change has got to come, when you follow God's plan for deliverance.

For more than four years I've worked at my little business in downtown West Michigan. For more than four years I had to struggle to pay a lease, try to get women to come for counseling, and take almost every penny to keep the doors to WomanSpace open. For more than four years I've worshiped in a black Baptist congregation where women in ministry are not respected. For more than four years the enemy has whispered in my ears, "Girlfriend, you ain't nothing and ain't going to ever be nothing!" For more than four years the enemy of my soul has sought multiple ways to entrap me, bring me down, and put out the fire and passion in my spirit. For more than four years it's been painful, very painful. For more than four years it's been disappointing, very disappointing. But, the Holy Spirit kept whispering within my spirit, "God said, Girlfriend, work the plan. God said, Sista, work the plan. God said, while it hurts like hell, build houses and invest in the midst of your captivity. Multiply and don't decrease. Don't you let the devil take your joy and make you stifle the gifts I've given you."

So, my husband and I have paid the lease at WomanSpace monthly, somehow! We are continuing to invest in West Michigan, where we live. Seek the welfare of your location. Plant trees. Plant shrubs. Plant flowers. Put your children in homes and schools where you live. Seek the welfare of your community. And pray for the heathens of your area. Pray for the very ones who want you to disappear. Pray their blessing. Pray their highest good. Pray their best benefit. For as we pray for them, God will lift us up, higher and higher. As we pray for their wellness and bless them, God will bless us, prosper us, and take us before those in authority so that we can be part of the system that will expose the evil one. As we pray for the welfare of the place where we are located now, our personal welfare is tied to it.

I can't run. Neither can you. God has not opened another avenue, somewhere else for us to escape. But, like our Savior, who went to Calvary as a captured criminal, who looked down at those who were doing him harm and prayed for their welfare, we too have to forgive those ignorant snots and move on. Oh, we've not always been so good. We've done our own share of dirt. But somebody prayed for us. They had us on their mind and took the time to pray for us. Aren't you so glad that they prayed for us? Don't you pray that they continue to hold us in their prayers? For it's been a long time coming, but I'm persuaded, I'm convinced, I'm convicted, and deep down in my heart, I do believe . . . It's been a long time coming, but, I do know that our change is going to come! I guarantee you that this is mighty, mighty, mighty good news!

NOTES

PREFACE

1. Carol A. Newsom and Sharon H. Ringe, eds., *The Women's Bible Commentary* (Louisville: Westminster John Knox Press, 1992), 328.

2. DeWitt Jones, Kim Jones, and Ron Kenoly, "Use Me," © 1993 Deinde Music / Integrity's Praise! Music.

INTRODUCTION

1. Lucille Clifton, untitled poem "won't you celebrate with me" from *Book of Light* (Port Townsend, Wash.: Copper Canyon Press, 1993), 25.

2. Dietrich Bonhoeffer, *The Cost of Discipleship* (New York: Simon and Schuster, Touchstone Books, 1995), 44–45.

CHAPTER 3

1. Edwin Hatch, "Breathe on Me, Breath of God," 1878, in *The United Methodist Hymnal* (Nashville: United Methodist Publishing House, 1989), 420.

CHAPTER 4

1. Rick Founds, "Lord, I Lift Your Name on High," 1989 © Maranatha Praise, Inc.

CHAPTER 6

1. Gwynne Forster, *When Twilight Comes* (New York: Dafina Books, 2002).

2. Joel Osteen, *Your Best Life Now: 7 Steps to Living at Your Full Potential* (New York: Warner Books, 2004); Rick Warren, *The Purpose-Driven Life: What on Earth Am I Here For?* (Grand Rapids, Mich.: Zondervan, 2002).

3. Harry D. Clarke, "Into My Heart," 1924, in *The Faith We Sing* (Nashville: Abingdon Press, 2000), 2160.

4. Daniel Iverson, "Spirit of the Living God," 1926, in *The United Methodist Hymnal* (Nashville: United Methodist Publishing House, 1989), 393.

CHAPTER 7

1. *Woman's World*, 12/06/05, n.p.

CHAPTER 9

1. Author unknown, from Mountain Wings: Daily Inspiration by E-mail, issue 5217, http://www.mountainwings.com/.

2. Daniel Iverson, "Spirit of the Living God, 1926, in *The United Methodist Hymnal* (Nashville: United Methodist Publishing House, 1989), 393.

CHAPTER 10

1. Author unknown; found on various Internet sites, several of which credit James Bender with relating this story in his book *How to Talk Well: The Art and Science of Professional Salesmanship* (New York: McGraw-Hill, 1949).

CHAPTER 11

1. Author unknown, found on http://dailychristianquote.com/dcqchar acter.html.

2. Edwin Hatch, "Breathe on Me, Breath of God," 1878, in *The United Methodist Hymnal* (Nashville: United Methodist Publishing House, 1989), 420.

CHAPTER 14

1. Hanna More, "Christianity: A Practical Principle," in *Practical Piety*, 1811.

CHAPTER 15

1. Jennie Wise, "Hold to God's Unchanging Hand," written early 1900s. In public domain.

CHAPTER 16

1. Darlene Clark Hine, *Rape and the Inner Lives of Black Women in the Middle West* (Chicago: University of Chicago, 1989), 912.

2. Safiyah Fosua, "Remembering Coretta Scott King: April 27, 1927–January 30, 2006," copyright © 2006 The General Board of Discipleship of The United Methodist Church. Used by permission.

CHAPTER 17

1. J. California Cooper, *Family* (New York: Anchor Books, 1992), 1.

2. Harry Elston and Floyd Butler, "Going in Circles," released by the Friends of Distinction, 1969, RCA.

3. Cooper, *Family*, 28.

4. Ibid., 228.

CHAPTER 18

1. Susan Weitzman, *"Not to People Like Us": Hidden Abuse In Upscale Marriages* (New York: Basic Books, 2000).

2. Rebecca Emerson Dobash and Russell Dobash, *Violence Against Wives* (New York: Free Press, 1979), 45.

3. Weitzman, *"Not to People Like Us,"* 25.

4. Ibid., 230.

5. Sweet Honey in the Rock, "Run," from their 25th Anniversary CD. Words and music by Nitanju Bolade Casel © 1994 Clear Ice Music (BMI).

CHAPTER 20

1. Barry Mann and Cynthia Weil, "Just Once," 1981 © Mann and Weil Songs, Inc.

CHAPTER 21

1. Dorothy Norwood and Alvin Darling, "Somebody Prayed for Me," 2005, Kosciusko Music.

CHAPTER 22

1. Sam Cooke, "A Change Is Gonna Come," 1963 © Abkco Music, Inc.